101
GREATEST
COOKIES
ON THE
PLANET

ERIN RENOUF MYLROIE

Author of *2-Ingredient Miracle Dough Cookbook*

PAGE STREET
PUBLISHING CO.

PAGE STREET
PUBLISHING CO.

First published in 2020 by
Page Street Publishing Co.
27 Congress Street, Suite 105
Salem, MA 01970
www.pagestreetpublishing.com

Distributed by Macmillan, sales in Canada by The Canadian Manda Group.

24   23   22   21   20   2   3   4   5   6

ISBN-13: 978-1-64567-087-2
ISBN-10: 1-64567-087-2

Library of Congress Control Number: 2019957256

Cover and book design by Rosie Stewart for Page Street Publishing Co.
Photography by Ekaterina Smirnova
Food Styling by Natalia Akst

Printed and bound in the United States

DEDICATION

To Sailor, who has been stirring up butter and sugar
at my side for all her young life. I couldn't have written
a cookie cookbook without her daily input, eye for
detail, inveterate love for visual beauty, inspiration,
creativity and plain old hard work. Someday she will
need to write her own cookie cookbook, and I'll be
the assistant—someday when she isn't busy with one
hundred other marvelously creative ventures. There
are many wonderful things waiting for her, cookies and
otherwise, and I'm honored that I've had her in
my kitchen and my home for these eighteen years.
I miss her already, and she isn't even gone.

TABLE OF CONTENTS

INTRODUCTION

This book has all of my favorite recipes in it. There are no gimmicks, no stunts, no overly fussy steps—but no shortcuts either. These are the cookies (and some brownies and bars snuck in) that I bake over and over again—the ones that get packed in brown paper sacks for lunchtime desserts, the ones that get wrapped in tissue paper and placed in tins to be delivered to neighbors at Christmastime, the ones that my sisters call me to get recipes for, the ones that win blue ribbons at county fairs. These are the cookies that bring happiness to a winter of discontent, and peace to times that try the soul. The cookies that make any house, even a college apartment, smell like a loving home. These are the genuine cookies of my heart.

I read a story about Raggedy Ann when I was a little girl. It said she had a candy heart that said "I love you" sewn into her chest. I'm pretty sure if that's true about Raggedy Ann, then I have a cookie where my heart should be. It might not have words, but it definitely has chocolate chips.

Friends, thank you for letting me share my 101 very favorite cookies with you. It turns out that sharing cookies is like passing on something very special, very sweet and very personal. This has been a labor of love in every way—a journey that was made even more memorable by knowing that someone like you would be reading and baking along. Thank you for giving me this space, this warm (probably 350°F (175°C) warm from all the baking) and welcoming space to share my love of cookies.

Love, *Erin*

SOME THINGS TO NOTE BEFORE YOU BAKE

Even if my heart beats for baking cookies, I should tell you that I don't have much love for washing extra dishes. This is a result of having a Tuesday and Friday dishwashing night growing up with ten siblings and with only a four-year-old sister as my dishwashing "partner." I'm scarred. I will do my duty and wash what needs washin', but if I can make a recipe with fewer dishes, I'm going to do just that. You'll notice that most of my recipes can be made in one bowl. Follow the directions about when to mix well and when to mix gently, and your cookies will come out as good as—nay, better than—if you messed up your entire collection of mixing bowls.

As for leavening, baking soda and baking powder are two vital ingredients for getting some lift on your cookies. Did you know that Soda Spreads and Powder Puffs? Don't forget it, and don't make substitutions when it comes to leavening. The amounts should be just right to get you the correct thickness on each of your treats.

If you don't have unsalted butter lying about, then by all means use salted butter. Unsalted butter tends to be a little fresher since it doesn't last as long on the fridge shelf. It's in a steadier rotation. That's all. No big deal.

I use a lot of parchment paper when I'm baking. It keeps the cookies from sticking and helps to preserve a clean taste. Sometimes a baking sheet will have some residual flavor from whatever was on it last. I've had a chocolate chip cookie that tasted slightly of roasted onion. Not good. Just use some parchment, OK? Or keep one cookie sheet for only cookie baking. I always try this, but I have yet to succeed. My own cookie sheets are in an atrocious state from high temperature artisanal bread baking. I'll tell you about it in another cookbook someday.

Eggs should ideally be at room temperature, but don't let it stop you if you didn't plan ahead. Not critical. Unless you're making meringues. And do make one of the four meringues I've included in this book! I love them dearly.

Speaking of meringues—which are naturally gluten-free—you'll find some vegan and gluten-free recipes here. This book wasn't designed for the baker with special dietary needs, but instead for the baker who shares with all their friends, and some of those friends are going to be vegan, gluten-free or maybe just cutting back on calories at any given time. There are treats here for every baker, and every eater. Cookies should be as inclusive as they are delicious.

WHERE TO START?

You might get an idea of where to begin by looking at the lists below. Happy baking!

SEASONS

Spring

Strawberry Shortcake Cookie Pizza (page 32)

Lemon Shortbread Bars (page 64)

Strawberry Meringues (page 91)

Almond Sand Dollars (page 112)

Summer

Ooey Gooey Sea Salt S'more Bars (page 20)

Pucker-Up Lime Melt-Aways (page 72)

Caramel Coconut Cashew Cookies (page 212)

Old-Fashioned Walnut Cookies (serve with root beer floats) (page 147)

Lime-in-the-Coconut Cookies (page 199)

Autumn

White Chocolate, Maple and Hazelnut Biscotti (page 76)

New Orleans Pecan Praline Cookies (page 108)

Vermont Maple White Chocolate Cookies (page 127)

Soft Molasses Cookies (page 151)

Salted Caramel Apple Cookies (page 192)

Winter

Hot Cocoa and Marshmallow Sno-Cap Cookies (page 83)

Snow-at-Midnight Crackle Cookies (page 71)

Hawaiian Snowballs (page 124)

Classic Vanilla Meringues (page 155)

Mini Chocolate Chip Cuties (page 175)

EVENTS & HOLIDAYS

Valentine's Day

Natasha's Raspberry Crumb Bars (page 100)

Utah-Style Pink Frosted Sugar Cookies (page 27)

Cherry Cheesecake Bars (page 115)

Giant Red Velvet Cookies with Cream Cheese Frosting (page 31)

Cream Cheese Shortbread Half-Dipped Hearts (page 116)

St. Patrick's Day

Lucky Charms Cookies (page 176)

Grasshopper Meringues (page 36)

Brûlée Sea Salt Caramel Oatmeal Bars (page 75)

Mint Chocolate Avalanche in the Andes Cookies (page 99)

Easter

Carrot Cake Whoopie Pies with Cinnamon Cream Cheese Filling (page 119)

Orange-Frosted Carrot Cookies (page 208)

Lemon Meatballs (page 44)

Raspberry Ribbon Cookies (page 60)

White Chocolate Cadbury Egg Cookies (page 111)

NEW YORK CITY GIANT CHOCOLATE CHIP WALNUT COOKIES

About ten years ago my family and I started going to a famous bakery in NYC. Although the lines were out the door and the bakery was a long walk from the Theater District where we stayed, it was worth it because the cookies were always next level. We've been to the bakery dozens (even baker's dozens) of times, bringing friends and family with us, toting cookies on airplane rides home, and sometimes even paying the exorbitant shipping costs to send them to loved ones on the West Coast. It has taken a lot of trial and error—and delicious experimentation—to come up with a recipe that replicates the bakery's cookies exactly. Thank you to my daughter Sailor who finally got it just right! If you make only one recipe from my cookbook, let it be this.

Makes 8 giant cookies

1 cup (227 g) unsalted butter, cold

1 cup (220 g) brown sugar, packed

½ cup (100 g) granulated sugar

2 eggs

1 tsp salt

¾ tsp baking powder

¼ tsp baking soda

¼ cup (32 g) cornstarch

2¾ cups (343 g) all-purpose flour

2 cups (336 g) semisweet chocolate chips

2 cups (234 g) chopped walnuts

Put the butter in a large microwaveable bowl and microwave on high for about 20 seconds to soften—not melt—the butter. Stir in the brown sugar and granulated sugar. With a wooden spoon or an electric mixer, beat until light and fluffy. Add the eggs and stir until well combined. Sprinkle the salt, baking powder, baking soda and cornstarch over the dough. Stir or beat for 1 minute. Add the flour and stir very gently until just combined. Fold in the chocolate chips and the walnuts.

Shape the dough into 8 equal balls. I like to gather the dough into a giant ball and cut it in half, then divide it in half again, and then again to get 8 semi-equal pieces. Place the balls on a plate and chill, uncovered in the fridge, for 2 to 4 hours. If you chill the dough longer it will take just a few more minutes to bake, which is fine, but be ready to adjust your bake time.

While the dough is chilling, preheat the oven to 415°F (215°C). Line two baking sheets with parchment paper.

Transfer the dough balls to the baking sheets, spacing them out evenly. Bake one tray at a time on the center rack until the tops of the cookies are just starting to brown, about 11 to 13 minutes. You can rotate the pan if the cookies are browning unevenly. Let the cookies cool for 10 minutes on the baking sheet before devouring, or before moving them to a rack to cool completely. The cookies are at their very best after 10 minutes of rest when the chocolate chips are ooey gooey, but they will still be delicious after a few days. The chips will be set, but the cookies will still be soft and tender inside.

PEANUT BUTTER LOVER'S ULTIMATE PEANUT BUTTER COOKIES

Whenever I go out of the country, I get hit with an immediate and intense peanut butter craving because I know it's hard to find peanut butter outside of the US. When I was studying abroad in Israel, my longtime friend and mentor Chris Peterson sent me a 5-pound (20-kg) bag of Reese's Peanut Butter Cups. Chris has passed away, but I know she would have loved these. These cookies give you a triple shot of peanut butter since it's baked in the dough, loaded into the cookie in the form of peanut butter chips and drizzled on top.

Makes 24 cookies

COOKIES

¼ cup (57 g) unsalted butter, softened

1 cup (258 g) creamy peanut butter, not natural style

½ cup (110 g) brown sugar, packed

¼ cup (50 g) granulated sugar

1 egg

3 tbsp (45 ml) milk

1½ tsp (8 ml) vanilla extract

⅛ tsp salt

½ tsp baking powder

½ tsp baking soda

1 cup (125 g) all-purpose flour, plus more if needed

¾ cup (126 g) peanut butter chips

¾ cup (110 g) chopped peanuts

TOPPING

⅓ cup (86 g) creamy peanut butter, melted, for drizzling

Sea salt, for sprinkling

Preheat the oven to 350°F (175°C). Line two cookie sheets with parchment paper.

To make the cookies, in a large bowl, cream together the butter and peanut butter until light and fluffy. Add the brown sugar and granulated sugar and beat for 2 minutes. Add the egg, milk and vanilla. Sprinkle the salt, baking powder and baking soda over the top and beat for 1 minute. Add the flour and stir very gently, until just combined. The dough should be slightly sticky. If it's too wet, add a tablespoon (8 g) of flour at a time until the dough is the consistency of playdough. Fold in the peanut butter chips and chopped peanuts.

Roll a heaping tablespoon (14 g) of dough at a time to form balls. Place on the prepared cookie sheets. Flatten each cookie with a fork, making a crisscross pattern. Bake the cookies for 9 to 11 minutes, or until the cookies are very puffed in the center and just beginning to brown on the edges. Let the cookies cool for 5 minutes on the cookie sheets.

To top, drizzle with the melted peanut butter and sprinkle very lightly with the sea salt. Remove to a rack and let the cookies cool completely.

Variations: *At Christmastime I leave out the peanut butter chips and skip the peanut butter drizzle. I dip the cookies halfway into melted chocolate and sprinkle more chopped peanuts over the chocolate. It's like buying a holiday outfit for the office party, but for peanut butter cookies. Another option is to add chocolate peanut butter cups to the batter if you want a little chocolate.*

CHOCOLATE, PISTACHIO AND ORANGE BISCOTTI

These fudgy biscotti aren't as crunchy as the biscotti that you might be used to. While they are crispy on the outside, they're a little chewy on the inside, with a rich and decadent flavor from the hint of orange and the crunch of the pistachios. If you want to leave out the orange zest, add a teaspoon of vanilla so that the biscotti still have some depth of flavor. I love to make these when I'm craving brownies but want something a little lighter. With all biscotti, if you want to take them up a notch, just dip them halfway into melted chocolate.

Makes about 20 biscotti

½ cup (114 g) unsalted butter, softened

1 cup plus 1 tbsp (215 g) granulated sugar, divided

½ cup (44 g) cocoa powder

2 eggs

1 tbsp (10 g) orange zest or 1 tsp vanilla extract

½ tsp salt

½ tsp baking powder

½ tsp baking soda

2 cups (250 g) all-purpose flour

1 cup (123 g) shelled natural pistachios

½ cup (84 g) miniature chocolate chips

Preheat the oven to 350°F (175°C). Line a baking sheet with parchment paper and coat with cooking spray.

In a medium bowl, mix the butter and 1 cup (200 g) of sugar with a wooden spoon until light and fluffy, about 2 minutes. Add the cocoa powder and stir until well combined. Stir in the eggs and orange zest or vanilla. Sprinkle the salt, baking powder and baking soda over the top of the dough, stirring to combine. Very gently stir in the flour all at once. Add the pistachios and chocolate chips.

Divide the dough into two equal pieces. Shape each piece into a 10 x 3-inch (25 x 7.5-cm) flattened log. Place them on the baking sheet about 3 inches (7.5 cm) apart. Sprinkle the logs with the remaining sugar. Bake for 18 minutes, or until firm on the outside.

Remove the baking sheet from the oven. Lower the temperature to 300°F (150°C) and let the biscotti rest for 5 minutes. Using a serrated knife, cut the biscotti diagonally into 1-inch (2.5-cm) slices. Turn the slices onto their flat sides and line them up on the baking sheet. They can be very close together since they won't spread. Return to the oven and bake for 5 minutes. Remove from the oven and let cool completely on the baking sheet. The biscotti will keep for up to a week in an airtight container.

OOEY GOOEY SEA SALT S'MORE BARS

Confession number one: I like these better than actual s'mores. Confession number two: This may be the only recipe in this book that can be made entirely in the microwave. Although they are easy to make, they aren't a simple bar. They have all the things you love about s'mores—ooey gooey marshmallows, mellow milk chocolate and sweet grahams—but the flavor gets amped up with the graham crackers and graham cereal, melted chocolate and whole chips, and swirls of marshmallows, finished with a sprinkling of sea salt. Confession number three: I just ate two of these for breakfast and I'm not even camping.

Makes 20 bars

1 (10-oz [283-g]) bag plus 2 cups (100 g) miniature marshmallows, divided

2½ cups (420 g) milk chocolate chips, divided

6 tbsp (84 g) unsalted butter, plus more for greasing the baking dish

1 tsp vanilla extract

¼ tsp salt

6 whole sheets of graham crackers, cut into 1-inch (2.5-cm) pieces, crumbs OK

6 cups (240 g) graham cereal, such as Golden Grahams

Sea salt, for sprinkling

Place 2 cups (100 g) of the marshmallows and ½ cup (84 g) of the chocolate chips in the freezer while you work.

Place the butter, remaining chocolate chips and remaining marshmallows in a large microwaveable bowl and microwave on high in 1-minute intervals, stirring in between, until the mixture is smooth. Working quickly, add the vanilla and salt to the mixture. Stir in the graham crackers and graham cereal and mix until everything is well coated. Stir in the reserved marshmallows and chocolate chips. Give the mixture a quick stir—you don't want the whole marshmallows and chips to melt completely.

Lightly grease a 9 x 13-inch (23 x 33-cm) baking dish with butter. With slightly damp hands, press the mixture into the prepared baking dish. Sprinkle the top with the sea salt. Let the mixture rest until set, about 1 hour, before cutting.

OATMEAL SANDWICH COOKIES WITH SPICED MARSHMALLOW FILLING

These oatmeal cookies are so good on their own, but the whole world loves an oatmeal sandwich cookie with marshmallow filling. Adding some of the cookie spices to the marshmallow filling really enhances the flavor. I'm normally not fussy about cookie size, but I like to use a medium-sized cookie scoop here. The cookies are already craggy and varied, so having roughly the same diameter helps to keep the sandwiches even.

Makes 16 sandwich cookies

13 tbsp (182 g) unsalted butter, softened, divided

¾ cup (165 g) dark brown sugar, packed

1 egg yolk

1½ tsp (8 ml) vanilla extract, divided

1 tbsp (20 g) molasses

½ tsp plus a pinch of salt, divided

½ tsp baking soda

1 tsp cinnamon, divided

¾ tsp cardamom, divided

¼ tsp plus a pinch of cloves, divided

¾ cup (95 g) all-purpose flour

1½ cups (135 g) quick-cooking oats, pulsed in the blender for about 20 seconds just until coarse and slightly broken down

½ (7½-oz [213-g]) jar marshmallow fluff

1 tbsp (15 ml) milk, plus more if needed

¾ cup (90 g) powdered sugar

Preheat the oven to 350°F (175°C). Line two baking sheets with parchment paper.

To make the cookies, in a large bowl, with a wooden spoon, beat 10 tablespoons (140 g) butter and the brown sugar until light and creamy, about 3 minutes. Add the egg yolk, 1 teaspoon vanilla and the molasses, beating for 1 minute. Sprinkle ½ teaspoon salt, the baking soda, ½ teaspoon cinnamon, ½ teaspoon cardamom and ¼ teaspoon cloves over the dough. Stir for 1 minute, or until the spices are well incorporated. Gently stir in the flour and oats, until just combined.

Using a cookie scoop, form balls with about 1½ tablespoons (21 g) of the dough. Drop the cookie dough onto the prepared cookie sheets, leaving 2 inches (5 cm) of space between the dough balls. Bake for about 10 minutes, or until the edges are browned and the tops of the cookies look set and dry. You want a crispy, fully baked cookie since it will soften once it sits with the marshmallow filling. Allow the cookies to cool for 10 minutes. Transfer to a rack and cool completely.

For the filling, in a medium bowl, beat 3 tablespoons (42 g) of butter with an electric mixer until light and fluffy. Add the marshmallow fluff, milk and ½ teaspoon vanilla. Beat for 2 minutes, or until well combined. Sprinkle ½ teaspoon cinnamon, ¼ teaspoon cardamom, a pinch of cloves and a pinch of salt over the filling. Beat to combine. Add the powdered sugar, beating until a light, stiff filling forms. You can add more milk if it thickens too quickly, but you want the filling to be fairly thick so it doesn't ooze out of the cookies.

To assemble, frost the bottom side of half the cookies and sandwich another cookie on top of each. Store in an airtight container in the fridge for up to 1 week.

NUTELLA® LAVA COOKIES

Sailor and I got really excited about the idea of a Nutella-based cookie with a semiliquid center of warm Nutella. We worked hard on a few different versions until we got it just right. And then . . . I couldn't find where I had written up the recipe and we had to start again. It was actually a blessing in disguise because Sailor made a big batch of the final test-bake to bring to the cast of the local high school production of *Mary Poppins*. We have heard from a reliable source that in one scene of the play, when the characters were supposed to be quietly improvising conversation in hushed tones, the only topic of conversation was the Nutella cookies. These cookies are kind of famous around here now! Some might even say they are supercalifrag-alicious.

Makes 12 cookies

COOKIES

1½ cups (387 g) chocolate hazelnut spread, divided (I recommend Nutella)

½ cup (114 g) unsalted butter, softened

½ cup (110 g) brown sugar, packed

⅓ cup (66 g) granulated sugar

1 egg

1 tsp vanilla extract

1½ tsp (4 g) cornstarch

½ tsp salt

½ tsp baking powder

½ tsp baking soda

1½ cups (188 g) all-purpose flour

TOPPING

2 tbsp (32 g) chocolate hazelnut spread, warmed in the microwave to drizzling consistency (I recommend Nutella)

Powdered sugar

To make the cookies, line a glass dish with waxed paper. At least 2 hours before baking, scoop 1 tablespoon (16 g) of the chocolate hazelnut spread onto the waxed paper. Repeat until you have 12 dollops. Freeze for at least 2 hours, or up to overnight.

Preheat the oven to 350°F (175°C). Line two baking sheets with parchment paper.

In a large bowl, cream together the remaining chocolate hazelnut spread and butter. Add the brown sugar and granulated sugar and mix until light and fluffy. Stir in the egg and vanilla. Sprinkle the cornstarch, salt, baking powder and baking soda over the dough and mix well. Gently stir in the flour.

Remove the chocolate hazelnut dollops from the freezer. Shape the dough into 12 equal balls. Flatten each dough ball in the palm of your hand, press a dollop into the center of the dough and wrap the dough around so that no part is exposed. Place the cookie dough balls, seam side down, on the cookie sheets.

Bake for 7 to 9 minutes, or until just set on top. Once the cookies have cooled, drizzle the warmed chocolate hazelnut spread over the tops and sprinkle with powdered sugar. The filling is delicious warm, but the taste and texture are also lovely—and maybe even better—at room temperature.

Tip: *Keep some extra frozen chocolate hazelnut dollops in a zip-top bag on hand for when you want to bake this cookie.*

UTAH-STYLE PINK FROSTED SUGAR COOKIES

I moved from the Los Angeles area to Utah—in the bitter cold of January after spending a semester in Hawaii—for college when I was 18. I was amazed to see my roommates running to gas stations—and later soda and cookie shops—for fountain sodas and big, fluffy sugar cookies frosted with a thick layer of pink frosting. It's a Utah thing. It didn't take long for me to join in with my roommates for late-night runs to devour these tender, chubby pink cookies. No matter what state is home, homemade pink sugar cookies are always best.

Makes 24 cookies

COOKIES

1 cup (227 g) unsalted butter, softened

¾ cup (154 g) vegetable shortening or (180 ml) vegetable oil

2 cups (400 g) granulated sugar, plus more for flattening the cookies

2 tbsp (30 ml) sour cream

2 tsp (10 ml) vanilla extract

2 eggs

1½ tsp (9 g) salt

1 tsp baking powder

½ tsp baking soda

5½ cups (688 g) all-purpose flour

FROSTING

½ cup (114 g) unsalted butter, softened

1 tsp vanilla extract

¼ cup (60 ml) sour cream

⅛ tsp salt

4 cups (480 g) powdered sugar, divided

2 tbsp (30 ml) heavy cream or milk, plus more if needed

Red or pink food coloring

Preheat the oven to 350°F (175°C). Line two baking sheets with parchment paper.

To make the cookies, in a large bowl with an electric mixer, cream the butter, shortening and sugar until light and fluffy, about 3 minutes. Add the sour cream, vanilla and eggs, and beat for 1 minute. Sprinkle the salt, baking powder and baking soda over the dough. Beat for 1 minute. Add half of the flour and beat until just combined. Slowly add the remaining flour, being careful not to overbeat. Stop as soon as the flour is incorporated in the dough.

Shape the cookies into 24 large golf ball–sized balls. Arrange evenly on the baking sheets. Dip the bottom of a drinking glass into the granulated sugar and flatten the balls gently in the center, to about ¾-inch (2-cm) thickness. The edges should be ragged. Dip the glass in the sugar between each cookie and repeat until all the cookies are flattened.

Bake for 7 to 9 minutes, or until the cookies are beginning to become golden brown on the edges. Be careful not to overbake—they should be nice and soft. Let the cookies cool completely on the cookie sheets.

Prepare the frosting while the cookies are cooling. In a large bowl, with an electric mixer, beat the butter, vanilla, sour cream and salt until light and fluffy. Add 2 cups (240 g) of the sugar and beat for 2 minutes, or until well combined. Add the cream and food coloring and beat until combined. Add the remaining sugar and beat the frosting until light and fluffy, adding more milk as necessary. Frost the cooled cookies generously. To make them just right, frost only the centers to leave a ½-inch (1.25-cm) unfrosted rim to expose the bare, ragged edges. Now you've got a real Utah cookie!

HALF-DIPPED PEPPERMINT BARK COOKIES

I save these special cookies to make only during the holiday season. The flavor of peppermint candy canes with dark chocolate and white chocolate is the taste of Christmas. These cookies have a couple steps, and I think they are so much fun to make. I look forward to baking these on a chilly December afternoon, warm and snug inside the house, with Bing Crosby's "White Christmas" playing a little too loudly, and my family hanging around in the kitchen. That's even better than Christmas morning, in my book. There's no present that's better than baking in the kitchen with that special holiday feeling.

Makes 24 cookies

COOKIES

1⅓ cups plus ½ cup (307 g) semisweet chocolate chips, divided

½ cup (114 g) unsalted butter, softened

1 cup (200 g) granulated sugar

2 eggs

1½ tsp (8 ml) peppermint extract

¼ cup (22 g) cocoa powder

1 tsp baking powder

½ tsp salt

1½ cups (188 g) all-purpose flour

TOPPING

6 oz (170 g) white chocolate melting discs

4 peppermint candy canes, crushed

Preheat the oven to 375°F (190°C). Line two baking sheets with parchment paper. Line a cooling rack with waxed or parchment paper.

To make the cookies, in a small metal bowl set over a saucepan of simmering water, stir 1⅓ cups (223 g) of the chocolate chips until melted and smooth. In a large bowl, beat the butter and sugar until light and fluffy. Add the eggs and peppermint extract. Stir in the melted chocolate. Sprinkle the cocoa powder, baking powder and salt over the dough. Mix well. Gently stir in the flour. Add the remaining chocolate chips. Shape into balls with about 2 tablespoons (28 g) of the dough. Place on the prepared cookie sheets, about 2 inches (5 cm) apart.

Bake the cookies for 7 to 9 minutes, or until cracked in several places. Allow the cookies to cool on the baking sheets for 5 minutes before transferring to the prepared rack to cool completely.

To make the topping, warm the melting discs according to package directions. Dip the cookies halfway into the white chocolate and sprinkle the dipped portion with the crushed candy canes. Allow the cookies to cool until the white chocolate is set, about 1 hour. If you need to rush the cooling process, just put them in the fridge for a bit.

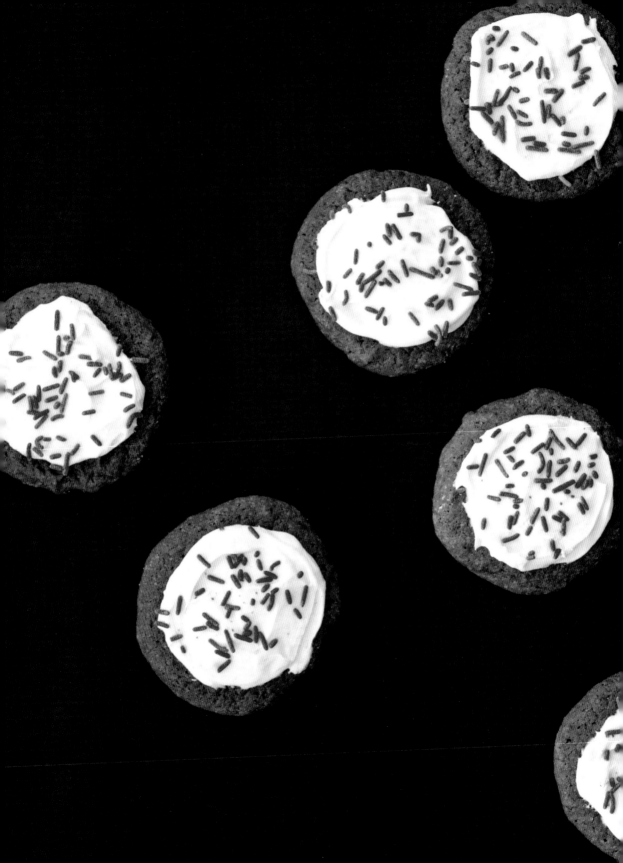

GIANT RED VELVET COOKIES WITH
CREAM CHEESE FROSTING

I wanted to make a special red velvet cookie for my sister-in-law. My idea was to stuff the cookie with cream cheese frosting. I got it all wrong. The filling was gloppy and hard to work with. I didn't add enough sweetener to the cream cheese, and although the cookies looked beautiful, they weren't the best. After a few attempts, I decided the very best way to make a red velvet cookie was just to keep it simple. This giant red velvet frosted cookie version is approved by all. They don't just look pretty—they're completely scrumptious! Don't skip the red sprinkles on top. They make the cookies extra inviting and they add a little textural crunch.

Makes 24 cookies

COOKIES

½ cup (114 g) unsalted butter, softened

½ cup (100 g) granulated sugar

½ cup (110 g) brown sugar, packed

1 egg

2 tsp (10 ml) vanilla extract

1 tbsp (15 ml) red food coloring

⅓ cup (27 g) cocoa powder

½ tsp salt

½ tsp baking powder

½ tsp baking soda

1¼ cups (156 g) all-purpose flour

FROSTING

4 tbsp (56 g) unsalted butter, softened

4 oz (113 g) cream cheese, softened

½ tsp vanilla extract

Pinch of salt

1 cup (120 g) powdered sugar

Red decorative sugar sprinkles, for topping

Preheat the oven to 350°F (175°C). Line two baking sheets with parchment paper.

To make the cookies, in a large bowl, combine the butter, granulated sugar and brown sugar, until light and fluffy. Add the egg, vanilla and food coloring. Sprinkle the cocoa powder, salt, baking powder and baking soda over the dough. Mix well until no lumps remain. Gently stir in the flour.

Shape the cookies into 24 ping pong–sized balls. Place on the prepared cookie sheets about 2 inches (5 cm) apart. Bake until set and starting to crack on top, about 8 to 10 minutes. Let the cookies cool completely before frosting.

Prepare the frosting by combining the butter, cream cheese, vanilla, salt and powdered sugar until smooth and fluffy. Frost the cookies and add the sprinkles on top.

STRAWBERRY SHORTCAKE COOKIE PIZZA

I'm not sure if it's a Utah specialty, but I know I had never tried so many strawberry desserts before living in Utah, including this pizza. It's like a strawberry shortcake in pizza form. It makes a beautiful treat to share for a baby shower, potluck or picnic. If you have homemade strawberry jam, it'll make this extra good!

Makes 12 big slices

COOKIE PIZZA

6 tbsp (84 g) unsalted butter, softened

½ cup (100 g) granulated sugar

1 egg

1 tsp vanilla extract

½ tsp salt

½ tsp baking powder

1¼ cups (156 g) all-purpose flour, plus more for the work surface

TOPPING

1 (8-oz [226-g]) block of cream cheese, softened

3 tbsp (45 ml) heavy cream or milk

½ tsp vanilla extract

½ cup (60 g) powdered sugar

2 cups (332 g) sliced fresh strawberries

1 cup (320 g) strawberry jam

Preheat the oven to 350°F (175°C). Lightly coat a pizza pan with cooking spray or line a baking sheet with parchment paper so you can create a free-form pizza. Lightly dust a work surface with flour.

To make the cookie pizza, in a large bowl, add the butter and sugar and beat until light and fluffy. Add the egg and vanilla. Sprinkle the salt and baking powder over the dough and beat for 1 minute. Gently stir in the flour. Transfer the dough to the floured work surface. Roll the dough into a 12-inch (30-cm) circle.

Transfer the dough to the pizza pan or baking sheet. Use your fingers to push the edges of the dough to create a built-up edge that looks like pizza crust. Bake the crust for about 18 to 20 minutes, or until set and just beginning to turn golden brown. Cool the crust completely.

To make the topping, in a medium bowl, beat the cream cheese, cream, vanilla and sugar until light and fluffy. Spread over the pizza, leaving the rim bare. Cover with the sliced strawberries. In a small microwaveable bowl, microwave the jam until warm and drizzle over the top. Let the pizza stand for 10 minutes before cutting into wedges.

MICHAL'S SWEET AND SALTY HELLO DOLLIES

My brilliant friend Michal makes the traditional layered bars—called Hello Dollies—with Ritz crackers instead of graham crackers. They're a potluck and bake sale favorite, since they're easy to make by simply layering the crackers with chocolate chips, nuts, coconut and other goodies. Bar cookies are always brilliant, since you can bake them up in one tidy batch, but these bars are extra brilliant because those salty Ritz crackers add balance to an otherwise strictly sweet treat.

Makes 18 bars

35 crackers, smashed into small crumbs, plus 8 additional crackers, crushed, divided (I recommend Ritz Crackers)

¼ cup (57 g) unsalted butter, melted

1 cup (168 g) semisweet chocolate chips

1 cup (168 g) peanut butter or butterscotch baking chips

1 cup (109 g) chopped pecans, walnuts or macadamia nuts

1 cup (186 g) sweetened shredded dried coconut

6 oz (180 ml) sweetened condensed milk

Preheat the oven to 350°F (175°C). Line an 8 x 8–inch (20 x 20–cm) or 9 x 9–inch (23 x 23–cm) baking dish with parchment paper.

In a large bowl, combine the crumbs from 35 smashed crackers and melted butter. Press the mixture into the bottom of the baking dish. Sprinkle the chocolate chips, peanut butter chips, nuts and coconut over the cracker layer. Drizzle the condensed milk over the top, trying to make it reasonably even. I use a spoon and slowly drizzle the milk, spoonful by slow spoonful. Sprinkle the remaining crushed crackers over the top of the milk.

Bake for about 25 minutes, or until the coconut is golden brown and the edges are nicely toasted. Let the bars cool for at least an hour. Cut into small triangles by first cutting 9 squares, then cutting each square in half on the diagonal to get 18 triangles. Store the bars in the fridge.

Tip: *You can double this recipe in a 9 x 13–inch (23 x 33–cm) pan. Sometimes it's best to double if you don't want a half of a can of sweetened condensed milk in your fridge. Sometimes it's best to double if you want to share with friends.*

GRASSHOPPER MERINGUES (GF)

I got on a meringue kick a few years ago and I couldn't stop making them. Before that, I didn't even know I liked meringues since I tended to skip them on cookie trays. I tried one once at a party, and I was hooked! This variation is based on grasshopper pie, the fluffy mint cream pie with a chocolate crust. The meringues will be light little pillows of mint, with the bottom dipped in chocolate candy coating.

Makes 36 meringues

2 large egg whites, room temperature

¼ tsp salt

¼ tsp cream of tartar

¼ tsp peppermint extract

Green food coloring, optional

½ cup (100 g) granulated sugar

1 cup (168 g) gluten-free chocolate candy melt discs, or 6 oz (170 g) chocolate almond bark

Preheat the oven to 250°F (120°C). Line a baking sheet with parchment paper.

In a large bowl, with an electric mixer, beat the egg whites until foamy. Add the salt, cream of tartar and peppermint extract. If using the food coloring, add about 9 drops to get a pretty light green color. Beat until soft peaks form. Add the sugar, 1 tablespoon (15 g) at a time, and continue beating until stiff peaks form. I like to lift up the beater and turn it upside down above the bowl. The mixture should come off the beater and stand up straight, not fall to the side. Beating the egg whites takes a bit of time— sometimes up to 10 minutes—so be patient.

Spoon the meringue onto the cookie sheet in heaping spoonfuls. Alternately, you can pipe the meringues directly onto the cookie sheet using a small-tipped piping bag. Either way, you should have about 36 meringues. They won't spread very much, so you can place them with just about an inch (2.5 cm) of space between on the baking sheet.

Bake the meringues for 45 minutes. Turn off the oven and let the meringues sit in the oven to dry out for 90 minutes. Remove from the oven and allow to cool completely.

When the meringues are cool, melt the chocolate in a microwaveable bowl on high power, stirring every 30 seconds, until melted and smooth. Dip the meringue bottoms into the chocolate and place back on the same parchment-lined cookie sheets. Repeat the process until all the meringues are dipped.

Let cool completely to set the chocolate, about 1 hour.

Variation: *If you want to skip the dipping of the meringues, add ¼ cup (42 g) of miniature chocolate chips to the meringue mixture just before piping onto the cookie sheet.*

SUPERSOFT PUDDIN' TAME CHOCOLATE CHIP COOKIES

These cookies have an incredibly soft and velvety texture, thanks to the addition of instant pudding mix. They remind me of the little poem my dad used to say to me when I was a little girl that included the lines "What's your name? Puddin' Tame, ask me again and I'll tell you the same!" I am pretty sure my dad used to repeat this poem to me because I asked the same questions over and over again, especially during the movies. He still teases me about that—and I still ask questions during movies. Puddin' Tame, Puddin' Tame after all these years.

I probably don't need to say this, but it's not the prepared pudding that goes into these cookies; it's the dry, boxed instant pudding powder that you find on a grocery store shelf. I like to use either the vanilla or cheesecake flavor, but you could certainly try different flavors, from banana to butterscotch. These cookies are on the paler side, so they bake at a higher temp, resulting in a cookie with a golden brown coloring and a lovely, delicate crisp top.

Makes 24 cookies

1 cup (227 g) unsalted butter, softened

1½ cups (300 g) granulated sugar

1 (3.4-oz [100-g]) box vanilla or cheesecake flavor instant pudding mix

2 eggs

2 tsp (10 ml) vanilla extract

1 tsp salt

1 tsp baking powder

1 tsp baking soda

2½ cups (313 g) all-purpose flour

2 cups (336 g) semisweet chocolate chips

Preheat the oven to 400°F (205°C). Line two baking sheets with parchment paper.

In a large bowl, cream together the butter and sugar until light and fluffy. Stir in the pudding mix. Add the eggs and vanilla. Sprinkle the salt, baking powder and baking soda over the top and mix well. Gently stir in the flour. Fold in the chocolate chips.

Shape the dough into generous 1-inch (2.5-cm) balls and place on the prepared cookie sheets about 2 inches (5 cm) apart. Bake for 7 to 9 minutes, or until the cookies are nicely golden brown on top. Let cool on the baking sheets for 5 minutes before transferring to a rack to cool completely.

CHOCOLATE PEANUT BUTTER MOUNTAIN COOKIES

These are big cookies—so big in fact that I like to cut them into wedges like a pie. Each cookie mountain is crammed full of peanut butter and chocolate chips. Want to add nuts? Go for it. Throw in ¾ cup (110 g) of salted, dry roasted peanuts. If you want your cookies to have a very dark appearance, use dark cocoa powder. And if you are a serious chocoholic (Me! Me!), try using dark cocoa powder, dark chocolate chips and walnuts instead of regular cocoa powder, peanut butter and semisweet chips.

Makes 8 giant cookies

1 cup (227 g) unsalted butter

1 cup (220 g) brown sugar, packed

½ cup (100 g) granulated sugar

2 eggs

½ cup (44 g) cocoa powder

½ tsp salt

1 tsp baking soda

½ cup (64 g) cornstarch

2 cups (250 g) all-purpose flour

1 cup (168 g) peanut butter chips

½ cup (84 g) semisweet chocolate chips

Preheat the oven to 415°F (215°C). Line two baking sheets with parchment paper.

In a large microwaveable bowl, heat the butter at full power to soften slightly for 30 seconds. Add the brown sugar and granulated sugar, and cream until light and fluffy. Stir in the eggs until well mixed. Sprinkle the cocoa powder, salt and baking soda over the dough, stirring until there are no lumps. Gently mix in the cornstarch and flour. Fold in the peanut butter chips and chocolate chips.

Divide the dough into 8 baseball-sized balls. Place the balls on a plate and chill in the fridge for about 15 minutes. Divide the dough balls equally between the cookie sheets. Bake for 8 to 10 minutes, or until the tops seem just set, even though the cookie will be very soft. Let the cookies cool on the baking sheets for at least 15 minutes before eating.

MAPLE-PECAN SHORTBREAD

When the evenings cool down after long, hot summer days, I'm ready for everything to take a flavorful turn towards autumn. Even shortbread gets a fall makeover at my house. These cookies have a beautiful caramel-y, maple-y flavor with a delicate richness from the pecans. They are so good all year long, but they are extra special in the fall. If you have apple tea to serve with the cookies, you will get an extra dose of autumnal cozy.

Makes 16 cookies

½ cup (114 g) unsalted butter, softened

½ cup (110 g) brown sugar, packed

¼ tsp salt

1 tsp maple or almond extract

1 cup plus 1 tbsp (133 g) all-purpose flour

¼ cup (27 g) chopped pecans, plus whole pecans for the tops

1 egg, beaten, for brushing

Coarse sugar, for sprinkling

Preheat the oven to 350°F (175°C). Line a baking sheet with parchment paper.

In a large bowl, cream together the butter and sugar until fluffy. Stir in the salt and maple extract. Gently mix in the flour to form a soft dough. Fold in the chopped pecans.

Gather the dough into a ball and flatten into a disc. Roll out the dough on a sheet of waxed paper to a ¼- to ½-inch (6- to 13-mm) thickness. Cut the cookies into 3-inch (7.5-cm) circles and place the cookies on the baking sheet. If you don't have a round cookie cutter, you can use the top of a drinking glass to cut the cookies. Brush the tops of the cookies lightly with the egg, sprinkle lightly with the coarse sugar and place a whole pecan in the center of each cookie.

Bake for 10 minutes. Let cool for 5 minutes before transferring to a rack to cool completely.

LEMON MEATBALLS

I've never seen these cookies anywhere but the Rochester, New York, area where my husband Shane grew up. We used to find them at our favorite neighborhood grocery store where we would buy them for dessert after a lunch of Italian subs. We still go back every year for lunch and cookies. The cookies are tender little yellow globes that burst with lemon flavor. The generous amount of baking powder helps the cookies keep their meatball shape.

Makes 30 cookies

COOKIES

8 tbsp (112 g) unsalted butter, softened

⅔ cup (80 g) powdered sugar

2 eggs, beaten

2 tbsp (30 ml) ricotta, plain yogurt or sour cream

2 tsp (10 ml) lemon extract

Several drops of yellow food coloring (I use 12 drops)

¼ tsp salt

1 tbsp (14 g) baking powder

2 cups (250 g) all-purpose flour

GLAZE

2 cups (240 g) powdered sugar

Juice of 1 large lemon

Yellow decorating sugar, for sprinkling

Preheat the oven to 350°F (175°C). Line two baking sheets with parchment paper.

To make the cookies, in a large bowl, cream together the butter and the sugar until light and fluffy. Add the eggs, ricotta, lemon extract and food coloring. Sprinkle the salt and baking powder over the dough. Mix well. Gently stir in the flour. Roll the dough into 1-inch (2.5-cm) balls. Place on the prepared cookie sheets about 2 inches (5 cm) apart. Bake for 8 to 10 minutes, or until just set. Let the cookies cool for 10 minutes before glazing.

To prepare the glaze, combine the sugar and lemon juice to form a thick glaze. Spoon over the warm cookies and sprinkle with the yellow decorating sugar.

PEANUT BUTTER AND
JELLY STREUSEL BARS

While I was traveling in Africa with my parents, my college-aged daughter Sailor
sent me a text with no words. It was just a picture of a bar cookie
with a golden-brown oatmeal streusel topping and an oozing layer of raspberry jam.
There were no words needed. I was in the middle of Kenya looking at a pride of lions,
but I stopped and texted back in all caps, "WRITE DOWN THE RECIPE."
A few minutes later I sent another text, "SAVE ME ONE." She did and she did.

Makes 16 bars

BARS

½ cup (114 g) unsalted butter,
softened

¾ cup (194 g) creamy peanut
butter, not natural style

1 cup (220 g) brown sugar,
packed

1 egg

1 tsp vanilla extract

¼ tsp salt

½ tsp baking powder

1½ cups (188 g) all-purpose flour

¾ cup (126 g) peanut butter
chips

1½ cups (480 g) seedless
raspberry preserves

TOPPING

½ cup (63 g) all-purpose flour

½ cup (45 g) old-fashioned oats

¼ tsp salt

¼ cup (65 g) creamy peanut
butter

1 tbsp (14 g) unsalted butter,
softened

½ cup (73 g) chopped dry
roasted peanuts

Preheat the oven to 350°F (175°C). Lightly grease a 9 x 13–inch
(23 x 33–cm) baking dish.

To make the bars, in a large bowl, cream the butter, peanut
butter and sugar until light and fluffy. Add the egg and vanilla.
Sprinkle the salt and baking powder over the dough. Mix well.
Gently stir in the flour. Add the peanut butter chips. Press the
mixture into the prepared baking dish. Cover with the raspberry
preserves.

To make the topping, in a medium bowl, with your fingers,
combine the flour, oats, salt, peanut butter, butter and peanuts
until the mixture forms large coarse crumbs. Crumble the
streusel over the top of the preserves. Bake for 22 to 25 minutes,
or until the top is golden brown. Let the bars cool completely
before cutting.

THREE-LAYER CHOCOLATE-GLAZED COOKIES

My mom used to make a version of this cookie at Christmastime, but the cream cheese filling was full of coconut, which I didn't like as a kid. Strangely enough, I did like nuts, which most kids seem to eschew. I used to beg my mom to make a few without any coconut, and she always did. Soon enough, it became the normal way to make them: without coconut and with a nutty filling. This recipe has been a family favorite that we've adapted throughout the years. Recipes are like that—if you hang on to them long enough, they almost always get so many tweaks that they take on a life of their own.

Makes 48 cookies

COOKIES

1 cup (227 g) unsalted butter, softened

1 cup (120 g) powdered sugar

1 egg yolk

2 tsp (10 ml) vanilla extract

½ tsp salt

2¼ cups (281 g) all-purpose flour

FILLING

4 oz (113 g) cream cheese

1⅓ cups (160 g) powdered sugar

⅛ cup (15 g) all-purpose flour

1 tsp vanilla extract

½ cup (55 g) chopped pecans

½ cup (59 g) chopped walnuts

GLAZE

½ cup (84 g) semisweet chocolate chips

2 tbsp (28 g) unsalted butter

2 tbsp (30 ml) milk

½ tsp vanilla extract

½ cup (60 g) powdered sugar

Preheat the oven to 350°F (175°C). Line two baking sheets with parchment paper.

To make the cookies, cream together the butter and sugar until light and fluffy. Add the egg yolk and vanilla. Sprinkle the salt over the dough and stir well. Gently add the flour. Shape the dough into 1-inch (2.5-cm) balls. Place the balls on the prepared baking sheets, about 2 inches (5 cm) apart. Using the handle of a wooden spoon, make an indentation into each cookie.

Bake for about 12 minutes, or until just light golden brown on the edges. Immediately press the handle of the spoon into the cookies again, to reinforce the indentation. Move the cookies to a rack to cool while you continue.

To make the filling, combine the cream cheese, sugar, flour and vanilla. Stir in the pecans and walnuts. Evenly divide the filling and spoon among the warm cookies.

To prepare the glaze, in a small saucepan, combine the chocolate chips, butter and milk over low heat, stirring constantly, until the butter and chips are melted. Remove from the heat and stir in the vanilla and sugar. Stir until smooth and then drizzle over the cookies.

CHOCOLATE CHIPPERS

A few years ago, my youngest sister Mary Kate called me as she was stepping out of a bakery with a bag of mini cookies. She had opened the bag and tried a cookie, and she immediately knew that we needed a way to make them at home. I hadn't tried the cookies yet, but she described them in detail: "They're fudgy, soft in the middle, crackled, full of white chocolate chips." "Mmm hmmm, mmm hmmm," I answered, taking it all in. Based on her description, I created a batch that night and then passed the recipe on to Mary Kate. Now this recipe has become as essential as traditional chocolate chip cookies in our families. You can make the cookies bigger, if you like, but I like the cute-as-a-button miniature size.

Makes 80 mini cookies

½ cup (114 g) unsalted butter, softened

⅔ cup (145 g) brown sugar, packed

⅓ cup (66 g) granulated sugar

1 egg

1½ tsp (8 ml) vanilla extract

½ cup (44 g) cocoa powder

½ tsp salt

½ tsp baking powder

½ tsp baking soda

1 cup (125 g) all-purpose flour

1 cup (168 g) white chocolate chips, plus more for poking into the tops

Preheat the oven to 350°F (175°C). Line two baking sheets with parchment paper.

In a large bowl, with a wooden spoon, mix the butter, brown sugar and granulated sugar until light and fluffy, about 3 minutes. Add the egg and vanilla and stir to combine. Sprinkle the cocoa powder, salt, baking powder and baking soda over the dough. Stir well, until there are no clumps of cocoa powder in the dough. Add the flour and stir gently. The dough will be very sticky. Add the chocolate chips. It will be a little messy since chocolate dough is sticky. Use your hands to form balls about the size of large grapes. Place the balls an inch (2.5 cm) apart on the prepared cookie sheets.

Bake the cookies for about 6 to 8 minutes, or until the tops are just set. Don't overbake—in fact, err on the side of underbaking. Remove from the oven and immediately put additional chocolate chips into the tops of the cookies. The cookies will continue to bake from the residual heat as they cool on the cookie sheets. Cool completely before serving.

FRENCH TOAST COOKIES
WITH MAPLE GLAZE

Years ago, we had a favorite donut place that turned out a French toast donut that we adored. There was a little bit of a textural crunch on the outside of the donut from cinnamon and sugar, with a maple glaze on top. It was scrumptious, especially because all of the donuts were made fresh to order. This also meant long lines and long waits, so the donut shop didn't last long. We had to recreate our favorite donut in cookie form. If you prefer the flavor of maple and bacon together, omit the step of rolling the cookies in cinnamon sugar, and instead sprinkle crisp bacon on top of the maple glaze.

Makes 24 cookies

COOKIES

¾ cup (170 g) unsalted butter, softened

2 cups (400 g) granulated sugar, divided

1 egg

1 tsp vanilla extract

1 tsp maple extract

½ tsp nutmeg

½ tsp salt

1 tsp baking powder

2¼ cups (281 g) all-purpose flour

1 tbsp (8 g) cinnamon

GLAZE

2 cups (240 g) powdered sugar

2 tbsp (30 ml) milk

1½ tsp (8 ml) maple extract

Cinnamon, for sprinkling

Preheat the oven to 350°F (175°C). Line two baking sheets with parchment paper.

To make the cookies, in a large bowl, cream together the butter and 1½ cups (300 g) of the sugar until light and fluffy. Add the egg, vanilla and maple extract. Sprinkle the nutmeg, salt and baking powder over the dough. Mix for 1 minute. Gently add the flour. Shape the dough into ping-pong-sized balls.

In a small bowl, combine the remaining sugar and cinnamon. Roll the dough balls in the cinnamon-sugar mixture and place on the prepared baking sheets, about 2 inches (5 cm) apart. Using the bottom of a drinking glass, flatten the cookies. Bake for about 8 to 10 minutes, or until the cookies are just beginning to set and turn golden brown on the edges. Let cool on the cookie sheets for 10 minutes before transferring to a rack to cool completely.

To prepare the glaze, combine the sugar, milk and maple extract to form a thick glaze. Spoon over the tops of the cookies and add a sprinkle of cinnamon. Let the cookies rest until the glaze is set, about 30 minutes.

CHOCOLATE-DIPPED COCONUT MACAROONS

I want to say that these cookies are a piece of cake to make, but that idiom might be a little confusing in a cookie cookbook. Instead I'll say that these cookies are a snap to make, but maybe that sounds like they're a ginger snap to make? I'll just say that these cookies are as easy as pie. Hee hee. I'll stop while I'm ahead, but no foolin', these cookies really are so easy to make.

Makes 30 macaroons

4 egg whites

1½ tsp (8 ml) vanilla extract

⅛ tsp salt

¾ cup (150 g) granulated sugar

2 cups (372 g) sweetened coconut flakes

2 cups (372 g) unsweetened coconut flakes

6 oz (170 g) semisweet or white chocolate, melted

Preheat the oven to 350°F (175°C). Line two baking sheets with parchment paper. The parchment is really important here! Don't skip it or your macaroons will stick to the pan.

In a large bowl, whisk the egg whites until foamy, about 2 minutes. Stir in the vanilla, salt and sugar. Add the sweetened and unsweetened coconut. Drop a tablespoon (14 g) of the coconut mixture at a time onto the prepared baking sheets, leaving a couple of inches (5 cm) of space between each one.

Bake for 20 to 25 minutes, or until the tops are lightly browned. Let the macaroons cool for 5 minutes on the baking sheets before transferring to a rack to cool completely. When the macaroons are cool, dip the bottoms in the melted chocolate and place them back on the parchment-lined baking sheets to set.

Variation: *OK, OK, one serious note. If you want to make these cookies taste like an Almond Joy candy bar, add ¼ teaspoon of almond extract with the vanilla, place one whole almond on top of each cookie before baking, then dip them in the semisweet chocolate when cool.*

WHOLE WHEAT
MILK CHOCOLATE CHIP COOKIES

Even when I'm not thinking much about healthy eating, I still prefer a healthy-ish chocolate chip cookie. I don't mean a low-fat, healthy cookie, but rather a good, hearty cookie full of nutritious whole grains and toasted nuts. With whole grains, I think just a handful or two of milk chocolate chips tend to taste a little bit better than semisweet chips since the sweetness of milk chocolate complements the heartiness of the whole grains.

Makes 24 cookies

½ cup (114 g) unsalted butter, softened

½ cup (110 g) dark brown sugar, packed

½ cup (100 g) granulated sugar

1 egg

2 tsp (10 ml) vanilla extract

½ tsp salt

½ tsp baking powder

¾ tsp baking soda

1 cup (120 g) whole wheat flour

1 cup (90 g) old-fashioned oats

¾ cup (126 g) milk chocolate chips, plus a handful more for the tops

¾ cup (88 g) chopped walnuts, plus a handful more for the tops

Preheat the oven to 350°F (175°C). Line two baking sheets with parchment paper.

In a large bowl, cream together the butter, brown sugar and granulated sugar until light and fluffy. Add the egg and vanilla. Stir in the salt, baking powder and baking soda until well combined. Gently add the flour and oats, and fold in the chocolate chips and walnuts. Roll the dough into 1-inch (2.5-cm) balls and place on the parchment-lined cookie sheets about 2 inches (5 cm) apart. Bake for 7 to 9 minutes, or until just set. Poke in the extra chocolate chips and walnuts—just a few! Get a big napkin and eat one warm.

OLD-FASHIONED BUTTERMILK FUDGE BROWNIES

My alma mater, BYU, contacted me a few years ago to do an article about my cooking for the alumni magazine. Even though I felt a little shy, I admit that I also felt awfully proud. I wasn't always the best student, so it felt like maybe I redeemed myself a little with my good work in the kitchen. I got to pick one recipe to share in the article, and I went with my buttermilk fudge brownies. They're my very favorite brownies, especially if you make them the night before and let them sit, uncut, so the chocolate flavor can develop. What I like best about these brownies is they somehow manage to be both fudgy and slightly cakey, which might seem contradictory, but it's somehow true. It's also true that not everyone considers a brownie a cookie, but for me, if you can hold a baked treat cleanly in your hand, it's a cookie.

Makes 12 large brownies

¾ cup (170 g) unsalted butter, plus more for greasing the baking dish

4 oz (113 g) good-quality unsweetened chocolate (I recommend Baker's in the orange box)

2 cups (400 g) granulated sugar

3 eggs

1 tbsp (15 ml) vanilla extract

½ cup (120 ml) buttermilk

½ tsp salt

1½ cups plus 3 tbsp (212 g) all-purpose flour, divided

1½ cups (252 g) highest-quality semisweet chocolate chips

2 tbsp (16 g) powdered sugar

Preheat the oven to 350°F (175°C). Lightly grease a 9 x 13-inch (23 x 33-cm) baking dish with butter.

In a large microwaveable bowl, combine the butter and unsweetened chocolate. Melt in the microwave on high in 1-minute intervals, stirring in between. Do not let the chocolate mixture sizzle—if it burns it can become bitter. As soon as the mixture is completely melted and smooth, add the granulated sugar and continue stirring until almost smooth. Add the eggs one at a time. Stir in the vanilla and buttermilk. Very gently add the salt and 1½ cups (188 g) of the flour. Stir until there are no dry flour spots and the batter is smooth.

In a separate small bowl, toss the chocolate chips with the remaining flour and fold into the batter. Pour the batter into the baking dish and bake for 28 to 33 minutes, or until a toothpick inserted into the center has just a few fudgy crumbs. Don't overbake—unless you like crisp edges—in which case go ahead and bake a little longer for more browning. Let the brownies cool for at least 30 minutes, but preferably let them sit at room temperature for at least 12 hours, before cutting. Dust with the powdered sugar before serving.

RASPBERRY RIBBON COOKIES

Although these are so easy to make, the pay-off is big. The cookies are crisp, delicate and buttery with a shiny dollop of jam and a sweet vanilla glaze. I like to make them all year, but I think they look their prettiest on a tray of Christmas cookies. You can use any type of jam that you like—I use raspberry, but blackberry would also be delicious.

Makes 30 cookies

COOKIES

½ cup (114 g) unsalted butter, softened

¼ cup (50 g) granulated sugar

1 egg yolk

1 tsp vanilla extract

¼ teaspoon salt

¼ teaspoon baking powder

1 cup plus 2 tbsp (141 g) all-purpose flour

⅓ cup (106 g) raspberry jam

GLAZE

½ tsp vanilla extract

1 tbsp (15 ml) milk or heavy cream

½ cup (60 g) powdered sugar

Preheat the oven to 350°F (175°C). Line a baking sheet with parchment paper.

To make the cookies, in a large bowl, cream together the butter and sugar until light and fluffy. Add the egg yolk and vanilla. Sprinkle the salt and baking powder over the top and mix well. Gently stir in the flour.

Divide the dough in half. Shape each half into an 11 x 3–inch (28 x 7.5–cm) log. Place the logs a few inches (7.5 cm) apart on the baking sheet. Make a ½-inch (1.25-cm)-deep impression down the center of the logs, about 1 inch (2.5 cm) wide. Bake for 10 minutes. Use a spoon to press down on the impression again and fill with the jam. Bake for 12 to 14 minutes, or until just beginning to brown. Let cool for 2 minutes. Gently transfer to a cutting board and cut the cookies on the diagonal into ¾-inch (2-cm) slices.

Make the glaze by combining the vanilla, milk and powdered sugar. Drizzle the glaze over the warm cookies. Let the cookies cool completely on a rack.

PEANUT BUTTER BALL-STUFFED CHOCOLATE COOKIES

When I was a little girl, there was a TV commercial with a kid eating a candy bar while watching a movie in the balcony of a movie theater. Below him, another kid is eating a jar of peanut butter while seated in the orchestra section. The kid above drops his chocolate bar into the jar of peanut butter below, and rather than getting frustrated that their treats are ruined, they decide to share and have a chocolate peanut butter treat. I loved that commercial because of the ridiculousness of the scenario. These cookies are kind of like that commercial. They have a creamy peanut butter ball wrapped up in a chocolate cookie. I like them to sit up tall and high, but if you want a more traditionally shaped cookie you can flatten the cookies out a bit with your hand before baking.

Makes 30 cookies

FILLING

½ cup (129 g) creamy peanut butter, not natural style

½ cup (60 g) powdered sugar

½ tsp vanilla extract

COOKIES

½ cup (114 g) unsalted butter, softened

1 cup (220 g) brown sugar, packed

1 egg

1 tsp vanilla extract

½ cup (44 g) cocoa powder

½ tsp salt

½ tsp baking powder

½ tsp baking soda

1 cup (125 g) all-purpose flour

Preheat the oven to 350°F (175°C). Line two baking sheets with parchment paper.

To make the filling, in a small bowl, combine the peanut butter, powdered sugar and vanilla until smooth and creamy. Roll the peanut butter mixture into 30 teaspoon-sized balls. Place the balls on a plate and chill in the freezer while you work on the cookie dough.

To make the cookies, in a large bowl, cream the butter and sugar until light and fluffy. Add the egg and vanilla. Sprinkle the cocoa powder, salt, baking powder and baking soda over the dough. Mix well. Gently stir in the flour. The dough will be sticky—and it will be a little messy to work with—but it will work! Form tablespoon-sized (14-g) dough balls and press each into a circle. Place a frozen peanut butter ball in the center and form the dough around it to encase the peanut butter ball. Place on the prepared cookie sheets about 2 inches (5 cm) apart. Repeat the process until you have 30 peanut butter balls wrapped in chocolate dough. Bake for 7 to 8 minutes, or until the top is set but still soft. Allow the cookies to cool completely on the baking sheets before serving.

LEMON SHORTBREAD BARS

Many recipes can benefit from a modern update, but these bars are not one of those. I want my lemon bars to be exactly the way they were when I ate them as a little girl: rich with a buttery shortbread crust, a luxurious, puckery tart custard filling and a sprinkle of cough-inducing powdered sugar. If you really can't help updating a recipe, just swap out the lemon juice for grapefruit or lime juice. Otherwise, just enjoy this well-loved lemony classic—just the way it was meant to be—since it's already perfect as it is.

Makes 18 bars

CRUST

1 cup (227 g) unsalted butter, softened

½ cup (100 g) granulated sugar

1 tsp vanilla extract

¼ tsp salt

2 cups (250 g) all-purpose flour

FILLING

6 eggs, room temperature

2½ cups (500 g) granulated sugar

Zest of 1 lemon

1 cup (240 ml) freshly squeezed lemon juice

½ cup (63 g) all-purpose flour

TOPPING

Powdered sugar, for dusting

Preheat the oven to 350°F (175°C). Line an 8 x 8-inch (20 x 20-cm) baking dish with parchment paper. Lightly spray with cooking spray.

To make the crust, in a large bowl, cream the butter and sugar with a wooden spoon until light and fluffy, about 2 minutes. Add the vanilla and salt and stir to combine. Gently stir in the flour. Press the crust mixture into the prepared baking dish. Bake the crust until it just begins to brown, about 16 to 18 minutes. Let the crust cool for 15 minutes.

Meanwhile, prepare the filling. In a large bowl, whisk the eggs, sugar, lemon zest and lemon juice until well combined. Add the flour and whisk until the mixture is completely smooth and no lumps of flour remain. Pour the lemon mixture over the warm crust. Return to the oven and bake for about 30 minutes, or until the bars are set. You can jiggle the pan to test. They are done when they no longer jiggle.

Let the bars cool for an hour at room temperature, then refrigerate for at least 2 hours, or up to 1 week. Before serving, dust the top with the powdered sugar and cut into squares.

MALTED WHOPPER® COOKIES

I've always liked Whopper candies. Even the name implies that the candy is
going to be a big, whopping treat—or maybe the name suggests a fib or an untruth,
as in someone just told a whopper. I knew someone that had the nickname "Whoppers"
as a child for just that reason. Either way, the malted milk candies are pure whimsical fun,
so why not make them into a light-hearted cookie? If you can't find malted milk powder
you can just sub all-purpose flour, but do try to find it because it adds a unique
toasty flavor that complements those big, giant, lyin' candies.

Makes 18 cookies

½ cup (114 g) unsalted butter, softened

¾ cup (165 g) brown sugar, packed

2 tbsp (30 g) granulated sugar

2 tsp (13 g) molasses

1 tbsp (15 ml) vanilla

1 egg

½ tsp salt

½ tsp baking soda

¾ tsp baking powder

½ cup (63 g) malted milk powder or all-purpose flour

1 cup (125 g) all-purpose flour

1 cup (168 g) chopped chocolate-covered malt balls (I recommend Whoppers)

⅓ cup (56 g) milk chocolate chips

Preheat the oven to 350°F (175°C). Line three baking sheets with parchment paper.

In a large bowl, with a wooden spoon, combine the butter, brown sugar and granulated sugar for 2 minutes, or until light and fluffy. Add the molasses, vanilla and egg and mix for 2 minutes. Sprinkle the salt, baking soda, baking powder and malted milk powder over the batter and stir for 1 minute. Add the flour and stir until just combined. Fold in the chocolate-covered malt balls and chocolate chips. Shape the cookies into 18 equal balls and place 6 balls on each of the prepared baking sheets.

Bake for 7 to 9 minutes, or until golden brown on top and just set at the centers. Let the cookies cool completely on the baking sheets.

ORANGE AND ALMOND SLICE-AND-BAKE COOKIES

I always make it a point to make my best Chinese dinners during the week of Chinese New Year. After dinner, I like to serve store-bought fortune cookies for the zany fortunes, but also these cookies because they are delicious. Since the cookies are slice and bake, I can prep them ahead of time and then bake them right after dinner. These may not be authentically Asian, but the flavors team up perfectly with the sweet and spicy flavors of Chinese food. They're crisp and only slightly sweet with an addictive orange and almond flavor. If you have any extra, these cookies are great for dipping in tea the next day.

Makes about 36 cookies

½ cup (114 g) unsalted butter, softened

¼ cup (50 g) granulated sugar

¼ cup (55 g) brown sugar, packed

1 heaping tbsp (10 g) orange zest

1 egg yolk

½ tsp almond extract

¼ tsp salt

¼ tsp baking soda

1¼ cups (156 g) all-purpose flour, plus more for the work surface

½ cup (54 g) sliced almonds, chopped

In a medium bowl, cream the butter, granulated sugar and brown sugar until light and fluffy. Add the orange zest, egg yolk and almond extract, and mix well. Sprinkle the salt and baking soda over the dough and stir to combine well. Gently mix in the flour. Fold in the almonds.

Lightly flour a work surface and shape the dough into a 12-inch (30-cm) cylinder. Wrap the dough in plastic wrap and refrigerate for at least 2 hours, or up to 1 week.

When you're ready to bake, preheat the oven to 400°F (205°C). Line two baking sheets with parchment paper.

Slice off generous ¼-inch (6-mm)-thick slices of cold dough. Place the slices on the lined baking sheets with about 2 inches (5 cm) of space between them. Bake the cookies for about 7 minutes, or until just set. Let the cookies cool for 5 minutes on the baking sheets before transferring to a rack to cool completely.

SNOW-AT-MIDNIGHT CRACKLE COOKIES

I've seen these cookies called by many names, but all of the titles involve the words crackle or crinkle. It's the most distinguishing feature of this gorgeous cookie, all dressed up in black and white formal wear. The cookie is rich and fudgy—thanks to melted chocolate and cocoa powder—with deep ridges of exposed midnight chocolate dusted with crinkly, crackly snow in the form of powdered sugar. It seems like the kind of cookie you should eat while reading "Stopping by Woods on a Snowy Evening," by the great American poet Robert Frost. "The woods are lovely, dark and deep, but I have promises to keep [. . .]" and cookies to eat!

Makes 16 cookies

4 oz (113 g) bittersweet or semisweet chocolate, chopped, or ⅔ cup (111 g) semisweet chocolate chips

4 tbsp (56 g) unsalted butter

¼ cup (22 g) cocoa powder

¾ cup (165 g) brown sugar, packed

¾ cup (150 g) granulated sugar, divided

1½ tsp (8 ml) vanilla extract

1 large egg

4 tbsp (60 ml) sour cream

¼ tsp salt

½ tsp baking powder

¼ tsp baking soda

1 cup (125 g) all-purpose flour

½ cup (60 g) powdered sugar

In a large microwaveable bowl, heat the chocolate and butter on high in 30-second intervals until melted. Using a wooden spoon, stir the chocolate and butter until smooth. Add the cocoa powder, brown sugar and ¼ cup (50 g) of granulated sugar. Stir until the dough is light and fluffy, about 2 minutes. Add the vanilla, egg and sour cream, mixing until all ingredients are fully combined.

Sprinkle the salt, baking powder and baking soda over the top of the dough, mixing until fully incorporated. Add ⅓ cup (41 g) of the flour at a time and mix very gently until just combined. The dough will be very sticky. Cover the bowl with plastic wrap and refrigerate for at least 2 hours, or up to 3 days.

Preheat the oven to 350°F (175°C). Line two cookie sheets with parchment paper.

Remove the cookie dough from the fridge and cut into 16 equal pieces. Roll each piece into a smooth ball. To finish, roll the balls first in the remaining granulated sugar and then in the powdered sugar.

Place the dough balls on the prepared cookie sheets, at least 2 inches (5 cm) apart. Bake on the center rack, one baking sheet at a time, until the cookies are cracked and puffy, about 9 to 12 minutes. The cookies should be slightly undercooked to maintain their fudgy texture. Let the cookies cool on the cookie sheet for at least 15 minutes before eating. Alternatively, you can cool completely, then store in an airtight container for up to a week.

PUCKER-UP LIME MELT-AWAYS

When I was a poor college student, my favorite cookie was a perfectly tart lime-pecan shortbread from an expensive kitchen store. I couldn't afford the cookies on a regular basis, but once in a while I would buy them as a splurge. My parents would also buy me a box for Christmas and birthdays. The cookies came in a beautiful green box, making them feel even more like a gift and a celebration. I would probably still be saving my pennies and buying those cookies, but the store stopped selling them and I had to figure out a way to make them myself. Over the last 20 years, this recipe has probably saved me hundreds and hundreds of dollars.

Makes about 28 cookies

½ cup (114 g) unsalted butter, softened

1 cup (120 g) powdered sugar, divided

Zest and juice of 1 medium lime

½ tsp vanilla extract

2 tsp (10 ml) lime extract

3 tbsp (24 g) cornstarch

¼ tsp salt

1 cup (125 g) all-purpose flour

¼ cup (27 g) finely chopped pecans, optional

In a large bowl, cream together the butter and ¼ cup (30 g) of the powdered sugar until light and fluffy. Add the lime zest and juice, vanilla and lime extract. Add the cornstarch and salt and stir until smooth. Gently stir in the flour. Add the pecans, if using. Shape the dough into a 9 x 1½–inch (23 x 3.75–cm) log. Chill the dough for at least 1 hour, or up to 1 week. If you chill the dough for longer than 2 hours, leave it on the counter for 30 minutes before proceeding.

Preheat the oven to 350°F (175°C). Line two baking sheets with parchment paper.

Slice the dough into ¼-inch (6-mm) rounds. Place the rounds on the cookie sheets about an inch (2.5 cm) apart—they won't spread too much. Bake for 10 to 12 minutes, or until just beginning to brown on the edges. Let cool for 10 minutes on the baking sheets.

Place the remaining powdered sugar in a bowl. Gently toss the warm cookies in the sugar, being careful not to break them. Remove the cookies to a rack and let cool completely. Toss in the powdered sugar one more time before serving.

BRÛLÉE SEA SALT
CARAMEL OATMEAL BARS

I like the idea of serving an Irish oatmeal treat on St. Patrick's Day, but this bar cookie is too scrumptious to only make once a year. The bars are so very good on their own, but I added the decadent broiled caramel topping to send them over the edge. My daughter Sailor especially loves any dessert with salt and caramel, so this is one of her ultimate favorites. The bars are at their very best when they are still warm from the oven and the top has a bit of crispiness from the broiler, but they are still very good the next day, as long as you cover them tightly with plastic wrap. Be sure to use Irish quick-cooking oats or regular quick-cooking oats for the most tender bars.

Makes 12 bars

BARS

½ cup (114 g) unsalted butter, softened

1 cup (220 g) brown sugar, packed

1 tsp vanilla extract

1 egg

1 tsp cinnamon

¼ tsp nutmeg

½ tsp salt

1 tsp baking powder

½ tsp baking soda

1 cup (125 g) all-purpose flour

2 cups (180 g) quick-cooking oats, preferably Irish

TOPPING

2 tbsp (28 g) unsalted butter, softened

⅔ cup (145 g) brown sugar, packed

2 tbsp (30 ml) heavy cream or milk

¼ tsp sea salt, for sprinkling

Preheat the oven to 350°F (175°C). Line an 8 x 8-inch (20 x 20-cm) baking dish with foil. Spray lightly with cooking spray.

To make the bars, in a large bowl, using a wooden spoon or handheld mixer, beat the butter and sugar until light and fluffy. Add the vanilla and egg and beat for an additional minute. Stir in the cinnamon, nutmeg, salt, baking powder and baking soda. Gently add the flour, followed by the oats. Press the mixture into the baking dish and bake for 22 to 26 minutes, or until the edges are light golden brown and the center looks set. Remove the oatmeal bars and preheat the broiler.

Prepare the topping by combining the butter, sugar and cream in a medium bowl. Spread the topping over the hot bars and place under the broiler until the topping is dark brown and bubbling, about 3 to 4 minutes. Watch carefully to make sure the topping does not burn.

Remove from the oven and sprinkle with the sea salt. Let the bars cool completely in the baking dish before removing and cutting into squares.

WHITE CHOCOLATE, MAPLE AND HAZELNUT BISCOTTI

Even though I generally prefer soft and chewy cookies, I make an exception for biscotti. I love their crispness and their light and crunchy sweetness. These twice-baked Italian cookies have an American twist with a beautiful hint of maple and cinnamon. I like the richness of the hazelnuts here, but you can also use pecans or walnuts with excellent results. If you're looking for a treat to package and send to a faraway friend, these biscotti travel very nicely.

Makes 24 biscotti

½ cup (114 g) unsalted butter, softened

1 cup (200 g) granulated sugar

3 large eggs, room temperature

1 tsp vanilla extract

1 tsp maple extract

½ tsp cinnamon

½ tsp salt

2 tsp (9 g) baking powder

3 cups (375 g) all-purpose flour, plus more for the work surface

1⅓ cups (153 g) coarsely chopped hazelnuts, plus more for the tops of the cookies, optional

3 cups (504 g) white chocolate chips

Preheat the oven to 350°F (175°C). Line a baking sheet with parchment paper.

In a large bowl, cream the butter and the sugar until light and fluffy. Add the eggs, one at a time mixing in between. Stir in the vanilla and maple extract. Sprinkle the cinnamon, salt and baking powder over the dough. Mix well. Gently stir in the flour. Fold in the hazelnuts. Cover the bowl with plastic wrap and refrigerate for about 30 minutes.

Divide the dough in half. On a floured work surface, shape each half into a loaf about 2 inches (5 cm) in diameter. Bake for 30 minutes. Let the biscotti cool for 10 minutes.

Cut the biscotti diagonally into ¾-inch (2-cm) slices. Place the slices cut side down on the same parchment-lined baking sheets. Bake for 8 minutes. Turn the slices over and bake for 6 to 8 minutes, or until golden brown. Transfer the biscotti to a rack to cool completely.

Place a medium bowl over a pan of simmering water, making sure the bottom of the pan does not touch the water, and melt the chocolate chips, stirring until the chocolate is melted and smooth. Dip the end of each biscotti in the chocolate and sprinkle with hazelnuts, if using. Transfer the dipped biscotti to a wire rack, set over a baking sheet, and allow the chocolate to harden. Store in an airtight container for up to 2 weeks.

PEANUT BUTTER CHOCOLATE MARSHMALLOW COOKIE PIZZA

My brother Roy got our family hooked on this cookie pizza one summer.
He found an old, beat-up pizza pan in the drawer underneath the oven and started
pressing in peanut butter cookie dough and topping with marshmallows and chocolate.
Never once did he make a real pizza in that pan, but then again, the only thing Roy
ever made was sweets. This one is a family favorite!

Makes 12 large servings

½ cup (114 g) unsalted butter, softened

1 cup (258 g) creamy peanut butter, not natural style

½ cup (100 g) granulated sugar

¾ cup (165 g) brown sugar, packed

2 large eggs, room temperature

½ tsp vanilla extract

½ tsp salt

1 tsp baking powder

2 cups (250 g) all-purpose flour

2½ cups (125 g) miniature marshmallows

1½ cups (252 g) semisweet or milk chocolate chips

Preheat the oven to 350°F (175°C). Lightly coat a 12-inch (30-cm) pizza pan with cooking spray, or alternately line a large baking sheet with parchment paper to make a free-form cookie.

In a large bowl, cream together the butter, peanut butter, granulated sugar and brown sugar until light and creamy. Add the eggs and vanilla. Sprinkle the salt and baking powder over the dough. Stir for 1 minute. Gently stir in the flour, being careful not to overwork the dough. Pat the dough into the prepared pan. If you're just using a baking sheet, use your hands to press the dough into a 12-inch (30-cm) circle. Poke the dough with a fork in several places so that it can release steam and not get too puffy in the oven. Bake for 15 minutes. Remove the pizza and sprinkle with the marshmallows and then the chocolate chips.

Return to the oven and bake until the marshmallows are toasty brown, about 4 to 5 minutes. Let the pizza cool for about 10 minutes before slicing. It'll be gooey and delicious.

SOFT PUMPKIN COOKIES WITH BROWNED BUTTER FROSTING

Pumpkin cookies are elevated to ambrosia here by a rich and creamy browned butter frosting. Each cookie is a bit like having your very own little pumpkin cake. As beautiful as they are delicious, they're just perfect for a chilly October or November night—even Thanksgiving night—since these are arguably more delicious than pumpkin pie.

Makes 24 cookies

COOKIES

½ cup (114 g) unsalted butter, softened

1¼ cups (275 g) brown sugar, packed

1 egg plus 1 egg yolk

¾ cup (180 ml) pumpkin puree

⅓ cup (80 ml) buttermilk

1½ tsp (8 ml) vanilla extract

½ tsp baking powder

¾ tsp baking soda

½ tsp salt

1 tsp cinnamon

1 tsp ginger

¼ tsp nutmeg

1½ cups (188 g) all-purpose flour

FROSTING

½ cup (114 g) unsalted butter, softened

Pinch of salt

3 cups (360 g) powdered sugar

6 tbsp (90 ml) heavy cream, plus more as needed

1 tsp vanilla extract

Cinnamon, for sprinkling

Preheat the oven to 350°F (175°C). Line two baking sheets with parchment paper.

To make the cookies, in a large bowl, beat the butter and the sugar until light and fluffy. Add the egg and egg yolk, pumpkin, buttermilk and vanilla, mixing until well blended. Stir in the baking powder, baking soda, salt, cinnamon, ginger and nutmeg. Mix well. Add the flour and stir until just combined. Using a ¼-cup (60-ml) measure, pour a little batter onto the cookie sheet and nudge it into a circle with the back of a spoon. Continue with the remaining batter. Bake for about 12 minutes, rotating halfway through, or until the cookies spring back. Allow the cookies to cool completely on the baking sheets.

Meanwhile, to make the frosting, melt the butter in a medium saucepan over medium heat. Cook, stirring constantly, until the butter is golden brown and you can see little flecks of brown in the butter. Watch carefully so you don't overcook. Add the salt and powdered sugar to the browned butter. Stir in the cream and vanilla. The frosting will thicken as it sits, so add more cream as needed.

Frost the cookies with the warm icing and sprinkle with the cinnamon.

HOT COCOA AND MARSHMALLOW SNO-CAP COOKIES

I love to bake these cookies in the winter on the same kind of cozy nights when I'm craving a mug full of hot cocoa. There is actual hot cocoa mix in the cookie dough, and the taste comes through as a sweet and mellow chocolaty cookie. If you want to get extra fancy, you could make homemade marshmallows for the tops of the cookies, or use purchased gourmet marshmallows in any flavor you desire. Whatever marshmallow you choose, just be sure to move the cookies to a rack after 5 minutes of cooling, or the marshmallows will flatten out. The cookies will still be delicious, but not as pretty.

Makes 24 cookies

½ cup (114 g) unsalted butter, softened

¾ cup (150 g) granulated sugar

2 (1.38-oz [37-g]) packets hot cocoa mix, without marshmallows

2 egg yolks

1 tsp vanilla extract

1 tbsp (5 g) cocoa powder

½ tsp salt

1 tsp baking powder

½ tsp baking soda

1½ cups (188 g) all-purpose flour

1½ cups (75 g) miniature marshmallows

1 (3.1-oz [85-g]) box semisweet chocolate candies covered with white nonpareils (I recommend Sno-Caps)

Preheat the oven to 350°F (175°C). Line two baking sheets with parchment paper.

In a large bowl, beat the butter, sugar and cocoa mix until light and fluffy, about 2 minutes. Add the egg yolks and vanilla and beat until incorporated. Stir in the cocoa powder, salt, baking powder and baking soda. Very gently stir in the flour. Shape the dough into 24 (1-inch [2.5-cm]) balls. Place the balls on the cookie sheets about 2 inches (5 cm) apart.

Bake for 5 minutes. Remove the cookies from the oven and press 5 or 6 marshmallows into the top of each cookie. Return to the oven and bake for 5 minutes. Immediately press a few of the candies into the marshmallows on each cookie. I like to divide them evenly, but make sure each cookie gets at least a couple. Let the cookies rest on the cookie sheets for 5 minutes, then transfer to a rack to cool completely.

WHITE CHOCOLATE–DIPPED GINGER CRINKLES

Do you ever get invited to those Christmas cookie exchange parties? I never know what to bring. Ironic, right? The best thing that ever happened to me at a cookie exchange was getting this gingersnap recipe. The cookies are gorgeous—full of deep crinkles and a sparkly sugar coating—but wait, there's more! These pretty Christmas treats are dipped in white chocolate and sprinkled with red and green sprinkles—like they're all wrapped up for Christmas. Look for holly sprinkles if you want to make these extra festive.

Makes about 36 cookies

¾ cup (165 g) vegetable shortening, softened

1 cup (200 g) granulated sugar, plus more for rolling

¼ tsp molasses

½ tsp salt

1 egg

1 tsp cinnamon

2 tsp (9 g) baking soda

1 tbsp (5 g) ginger

2 cups (250 g) all-purpose flour

8 oz (226 g) white chocolate melting discs, or white vanilla-almond bark

Red and green sprinkles

Preheat the oven to 350°F (175°C). Line three cookie sheets with parchment paper.

In a large bowl, cream the shortening and sugar until light and fluffy. Add the molasses, salt and egg, mixing until well combined. There should be no streaks of egg or molasses. Sprinkle the cinnamon, baking soda and ginger over the dough. Stir until well combined. Gently mix in the flour. Shape the dough into ¾-inch (2-cm) balls. You should have about 36 balls. Roll each one in sugar and place on the cookie sheets with 2 inches (5 cm) between each cookie.

Bake the cookies for 12 to 15 minutes, or until crinkled and puffed. Cool for 5 minutes on the cookie sheets. Transfer to a rack and cool completely.

Melt the white chocolate according to package directions. Dip half of each cookie in the chocolate and sprinkle the dipped side with the red and green sprinkles. Return to the rack and let the cookies rest until the chocolate is completely set. If you need the chocolate to set quickly, you can put the cookies in the fridge.

ANNA'S APPLE CRUMB BARS

This recipe comes from one of the best bakers and loveliest people I know, Anna Ginsberg of the blog Cookie Madness. Anna and I met at a cooking contest years ago. She was a cooking contest champion, which is no surprise at all. Anna sticks with a recipe and works it until she gets it just right, which I think is a hallmark of all of the best bakers. They don't quit until they achieve perfection. Anna generously agreed to share her apple crumb bar recipe for my book. I didn't even try to develop my own recipe because Anna's recipe is already perfect. I make it every September—and sometimes for Thanksgiving—since I think these bars are even better than pie.

Makes 12 bars

¾ cup (165 g) brown sugar, packed

¾ cup (68 g) old-fashioned rolled oats

1½ cups (188 g) all-purpose flour

⅜ tsp baking soda

⅜ tsp salt

10 tbsp (140 g) unsalted butter, cold, divided

2–3 small unpeeled apples, cored and thinly sliced or chopped (I use 3 small Granny Smith)

2 tsp (10 ml) lemon juice, divided

½ tsp cinnamon

½ cup (100 g) granulated sugar

1½ tbsp (12 g) cornstarch

½ cup (120 ml) water

½ tsp vanilla extract

½ cup (55 g) chopped pecans

Preheat the oven to 350°F (175°C). Line a 9-inch (23-cm) square metal pan with nonstick foil or parchment paper.

To make the crust, in a bowl or food processor, combine the brown sugar, oats, flour, baking soda and salt. Cut in or process in 9 tablespoons (126 g) of the butter until the mixture is coarse and crumbly. Reserve about ¾ cup (168 g) of the mixture for the topping. Pat the remaining mixture into the bottom of the pan. It will seem dry, but it's supposed to be.

Toss the apples with half of the lemon juice and arrange in a layer across the crust. Sprinkle with the cinnamon. In a saucepan over medium heat, combine the granulated sugar, cornstarch and water, and cook, whisking constantly, until the mixture begins to boil and thicken. Remove from the heat and stir in the vanilla, the remaining butter and the remaining lemon juice. Pour the mixture over the apples. Sprinkle the reserved oat crumbs on top, then sprinkle with the pecans.

Bake for 35 to 45 minutes, or until the top is lightly browned. If you prefer bars that hold together, let the bars cool completely and then chill before cutting. You can bring them back to room temperature after chilling, of course.

CHOCOLATE CHIP COOKIES (v)

I didn't write this cookbook specifically for vegans, but more for home bakers
that want to bring a plate of cookies to all the people they love. I have several people
that I like to give vegan cookies to, and this number is growing all the time. I also
wanted a vegan cookie that made no one feel they had to announce, "This is a vegan cookie!"
It had to be good enough for any type of eater to enjoy.

This might be the most tested recipe in the book. The best vegan chocolate chip cookie had
to first ditch the vegan butter, which tends to have an artificial aftertaste. Vegetable oil makes
a moist, chewy cookie that keeps well and has a clean flavor. It does require more vanilla and
salt for the best flavor. I also tried the recipe with a variety of egg substitutes—even water—
but my most consistent and neutral results came from using a flaxseed egg. If you don't want
to have flaxseed on hand you can substitute ¼ cup (59 g) of pumpkin puree, mashed banana or
applesauce. The flavor of the fruit will come through a bit, but it will be a delicious variation.

Makes 24 cookies

1 tbsp (7 g) ground flaxseed

3 tbsp (45 ml) water, hot

½ cup (120 ml) vegetable oil

¾ cup (165 g) dark brown sugar,
packed

¼ cup (50 g) granulated sugar

1 tsp molasses

1 tbsp (15 ml) vanilla extract

¾ tsp salt

½ tsp baking powder

½ tsp baking soda

1 cup plus 2 tbsp (141 g)
all-purpose flour

1 cup (168 g) vegan chocolate
chips, or 6 oz (170 g) vegan
chocolate bar, cut into pieces,
plus more for topping

½ cup (59 g) chopped walnuts

Sea salt, for the tops

Preheat the oven to 375°F (190°C). Line two baking sheets with
parchment paper.

In a small bowl, stir together the flaxseed and water. Set aside
for 10 minutes. In a large bowl, stir together the oil, dark brown
sugar, granulated sugar, molasses and vanilla. Stir in the reserved
flaxseed mixture. Sprinkle the salt, baking powder and baking
soda over the dough. Mix well. Gently stir in the flour. Fold in
the chocolate chips and walnuts. Vegan chocolate chips will
resist mixing into the batter. If any fall out of the dough, just
poke them back in before baking.

Roll the dough into balls using 2 tablespoons (28 g) of dough
each and place on the prepared baking sheets. Sprinkle with
the sea salt.

Bake until cracked and just beginning to turn golden brown
in places, about 7 to 9 minutes. Immediately poke the extra
chips into the tops of the cookies. Allow the cookies to cool
completely on the baking sheets.

STRAWBERRY MERINGUES (GF)

I've always heard it's not best to make meringues on a humid day, but since I live in the desert it's not usually an issue for me. I like to make strawberry meringues in the springtime anyway, when hot and humid times are far away still. These are like little pink clouds of strawberry-scented confection, with little flecks of crunchy dried strawberries inside. The best way to get the strawberry flavor while keeping the meringues dry is to use strawberry jello powder.

Makes about 40 meringues

3 egg whites, room temperature

Pinch of salt

¼ tsp cream of tartar

¾ cup (150 g) granulated sugar

3 tbsp (41 g) strawberry jello powder, directly from the box

1 cup (14 g) freeze-dried strawberries, chopped (even the dust after chopping is fine to add)

Preheat the oven to 250°F (100°C). Line two baking sheets with parchment paper.

In a clean, dry bowl, using an electric mixer, whisk the egg whites until foamy. Add the salt and cream of tartar. Continue to beat the egg whites, adding the sugar, until stiff peaks form. This usually takes between 5 and 7 minutes. Add the jello powder and beat for 1 minute. Fold in the strawberries. Drop the meringues by heaping spoonfuls onto the prepared baking sheets, leaving an inch (2.5 cm) of space between them. You should have about 40 meringues.

Bake for 45 minutes. Open the oven and lightly touch the top of a meringue. It should be dry. If it's still moist, close the oven and bake for 2 minutes longer, repeating this process until the meringues are dry to the touch. Turn off the oven and let the meringues sit in the oven to dry out for an hour. Remove to a rack and allow the meringues to cool completely.

CLASSIC BLONDIES

I adore blondies, but alas, I'm very picky about them. Oh OK, I'm picky about everything. I admit it. I hope you'll love me anyway. Blondies have to be just right. They must have lots of brown sugar, more than a hint of vanilla, plenty of irregular bumps and crags from the perfect amount of chips and nuts and—this is maybe the most important—a moist, chewy texture. It's really easy to dry out the edges on blondies in order to make sure the center is baked. I think it's better to err on the side of underdone in the center to protect the integrity of the chewy edges. Besides, the blondies will continue to bake from residual heat when you take them out of the oven, so don't wait until the center is perfect. Just follow my baking directions below and have patience in the cooling process (can you wait overnight?), and they'll come out perfect. I like to make a small batch of blondies in a square baking dish for the best results, but you can also double the recipe and bake it in a 9 x 13-inch (23 x 33-cm) baking dish. If you want a really large batch, and one that bakes beautifully every time, try quadrupling (yep—quadrupling!) the batch and baking it in a rimmed 13 x 18-inch (33 x 46-cm) half-sheet pan.

Makes 9 cookies

6 tbsp (84 g) unsalted butter, cold, plus more for greasing the pan

1 cup (220 g) brown sugar, packed

2½ tsp (13 ml) vanilla extract

1 egg

½ tsp salt

¾ tsp baking powder

1 cup (125 g) all-purpose flour

½ cup (84 g) semisweet chocolate chips

½ cup (55 g) finely chopped pecans, toasted

Preheat the oven to 350°F (175°C). Lightly grease an 8 x 8-inch (20 x 20-cm) or 9 x 9-inch (23 x 23-cm) baking dish.

In a large microwaveable bowl, heat the butter on high for 20 seconds. Cream the butter and sugar together until light and fluffy. Add the vanilla and egg. Sprinkle the salt and baking powder over the dough. Stir until well mixed. Very gently stir in the flour. Fold in the chocolate chips and pecans. Spread the batter into the prepared baking dish.

Bake for 26 to 28 minutes. To check for doneness, poke a toothpick into the edge. It should come out dry. Poke a toothpick 2 inches (5 cm) away from the edge, and you should have moist crumbs. The top should be set and puffed and the edges should be a rich, golden brown while the center is a pale, golden brown. Place the blondies on a rack and allow them to cool for at least 2 hours, or even better, overnight. An overnight rest will only enhance the flavor. They're still setting as they cool, so don't cut in! They will sink a little bit, but that's normal. They're going to be rich and chewy and buttery.

DARK CHOCOLATE–DIPPED PUMPKIN BISCOTTI

Back in my blogging days I used to host an annual October event called "Cookie Bookie" wherein I would share a cookie recipe and a review of a spooky novel. Even now, over a decade later, it's the part of my blog that is the most mentioned and the most missed. I still get October emails asking me to bring back Cookie Bookie. Maybe someday I will! Until then, please find a spooky novel to read and make a batch of these Dark Chocolate–Dipped Pumpkin Biscotti to enjoy, snuggled in against the cold, knowing you are perfectly safe while you read and munch in fear.

Makes 20 biscotti

3 tbsp (42 g) unsalted butter, softened

½ cup (100 g) granulated sugar

⅓ cup (80 ml) pumpkin puree

1 egg

⅛ tsp salt

¾ tsp baking powder

¼ tsp baking soda

½ tsp ginger

½ tsp cinnamon

½ cup (63 g) all-purpose flour, plus more for assembling the dough

¾ cup (90 g) whole wheat flour

6 oz (170 g) bittersweet or semisweet chocolate, melted, for dipping

½ cup (69 g) pepitas (shelled pumpkin seeds)

Preheat the oven to 350°F (175°C). Line a baking sheet with parchment paper.

In a large bowl, cream together the butter and sugar until light and fluffy. Stir in the pumpkin and egg. Sprinkle the salt, baking powder, baking soda, ginger and cinnamon over the dough. Stir vigorously for 1 minute. Gently mix in the all-purpose flour and whole wheat flour until just combined. The dough will be sticky. Using a generous amount of flour on your hands, shape the dough into a 1½ x 15–inch (3.75 x 38–cm) log. Bake the log for 15 minutes. Cool for 20 minutes.

Gently cut the biscotti into ¾-inch (2-cm) slices with a serrated knife. Place on the cookie sheet, cut side down. Bake for 15 minutes, or until firm. When the biscotti are cool, dip them halfway into the melted chocolate and sprinkle the chocolate with the pepitas. Let the chocolate harden and grab your spooky novel.

MIKE'S URBAN COWBOY COOKIES

I named these cookies after my brother-in-law Mike. I shouldn't even call him a brother "in-law" since I've known him since I was a kid and he has always felt like a real older brother to me. Mike had always lived in Los Angeles, but just recently he and my sister Leslie bought a house in the country. Mike promptly got himself a cowboy hat to wear around town on the weekends. He likes his hat so much that he even wears it inside the house. Leslie caught him ironing his city slicker, button-down work shirt in his cowboy hat. Now, you may have heard of cowboy cookies, but these are cowboy cookies on steroids. They've got all kinds of both sophisticated and down-to-earth mix ins, like chocolate-covered pretzels, corn chips, coconut and nuts. These cookies are for you, Urban Cowboy Mike.

Makes about 24 cookies

1 cup (227 g) unsalted butter, softened

1 cup (220 g) brown sugar, packed

¾ cup (150 g) granulated sugar

2 eggs

1 tbsp (15 ml) vanilla extract

½ tsp coconut extract, optional

1 tsp salt

1 tsp baking powder

1 tsp baking soda

2½ cups (313 g) all-purpose flour

½ cup (45 g) old-fashioned oats

1 cup (60 g) coarsely crushed chocolate-covered pretzels, plus more whole pretzels to poke into the tops

1 cup (66 g) coarsely crushed deep-fried corn chips (I recommend Fritos)

¾ cup (70 g) unsweetened coconut flakes, toasted

¾ cup (82 g) chopped candied or toasted pecans

Preheat the oven to 350°F (175°C). Line two baking sheets with parchment paper.

In a large bowl, using an electric mixer or a wooden spoon, cream the butter, brown sugar and granulated sugar until light and fluffy. Add the eggs, vanilla and coconut extract, if using, stirring until well combined. Sprinkle the salt, baking powder and baking soda over the batter and stir to combine. Add the flour in all at once and gently stir. Fold in the oats, pretzels, chips, coconut flakes and pecans. Roll the dough into 3-tablespoon (42-g)-sized balls.

Bake for 10 to 12 minutes, or until just set and golden brown on top. Poke the additional pretzels into the tops of the cookies. Let the cookies cool completely on the cookie sheets before eating. Store in an airtight container for up to 1 week.

MINT CHOCOLATE AVALANCHE IN THE ANDES COOKIES

My son West is a maniac for mint and chocolate. His favorite ice cream is mint chocolate chip, his favorite Oreo is mint chocolate and his favorite candy is Andes mints. I wanted to create a cookie that would be an explosion of all of West's favorite mint and chocolate–flavored treats. These might be a little over the top, but so is West's love of mint-and-chocolate, so maybe they're actually proportional.

Makes 24 cookies

1 cup (227 g) unsalted butter, softened

1½ cups (330 g) light brown sugar, packed

½ cup (100 g) granulated sugar

2 eggs

1 tsp vanilla extract

1½ tsp (8 ml) peppermint extract (do not use any other type of mint extract but peppermint)

1 tsp salt

1½ tsp (7 g) baking powder

½ tsp baking soda

¾ cup (66 g) cocoa powder

2 cups (250 g) all-purpose flour

1 cup (86 g) coarsely crushed mint cream–filled chocolate sandwich cookies, plus more for poking into the tops (I recommend Mint Oreos)

1 cup (120 g) mint chocolate candies, chopped, plus more for poking into the tops (I recommend Andes Mints)

1 cup (168 g) candy-coated mint chocolates, plus more for poking into the tops (I recommend Mint M&M's)

1 cup (168 g) mint or semisweet chocolate chips

Preheat the oven to 350°F (175°C). Line two baking sheets with parchment paper.

In a large bowl, using an electric mixer or a wooden spoon, cream the butter, brown sugar and granulated sugar until light and fluffy. Add the eggs, vanilla and peppermint extract, stirring until well combined. Sprinkle the salt, baking powder, baking soda and cocoa powder over the batter. Stir until no lumps of cocoa powder remain. Add the flour in all at once and gently stir to combine. The dough will be sticky. Fold in the cookies, mint chocolate candies, candy-coated mint chocolates and chocolate chips until distributed throughout the dough. Roll the dough into 3-tablespoon (42-g)-sized balls and place on the baking sheets.

Bake for 9 to 12 minutes, or until just set and almost firm. Do not overbake.

Immediately poke more cookies, mint chocolate candies and candy-coated mint chocolates into the tops of the cookies. The cookies will continue to bake from the residual heat as they cool completely on the baking sheets. Let them rest until cooled, about 30 minutes, before eating.

NATASHA'S RASPBERRY CRUMB BARS

When my sister-in-law Natasha came for a weekend visit to attend my daughter Sailor's baby blessing, she brought my mother a plate of homemade raspberry chocolate crumb bars. It was a lovely gesture. My mother wrote the ingredients for the recipe on a sheet of paper and tucked it away into her recipe book. There was no title on the recipe, but my mother wrote the name NATASHA in beautiful cursive with a pink pencil and decorated the top of the paper with little pink hearts. I think it's safe to say that my mother loved both Natasha (everyone does!) and the raspberry bars (everyone loves those too).

P.S. Try these sometime with white chocolate instead of semisweet chips.

Makes 9 bars

1 cup (125 g) all-purpose flour

1 cup (90 g) quick-cooking oats

⅔ cup (145 g) brown sugar, packed

¼ tsp baking soda

½ tsp salt

½ cup (114 g) unsalted butter, softened

1 cup (320 g) raspberry jam

¾ cup (126 g) semisweet chocolate chips

¼ cup (27 g) chopped pecans

Preheat the oven to 350°F (175°C). Line an 8 x 8–inch (20 x 20–cm) or 9 x 9–inch (23 x 23–cm) baking dish with parchment paper, allowing some parchment to hang slightly over the edge of the pan to create handles for removing the bars later.

In a large bowl, stir together the flour, oats, sugar, baking soda and salt. Using your fingertips, rub the butter into the flour mixture until you have irregular-sized coarse crumbs, about the size of peas. Reserve ½ cup (112 g) of the mixture. Press the rest of the mixture into the bottom of the baking dish. Spread the jam over the crumbs in the baking dish and scatter the chocolate chips over the jam. Add the pecans to the reserved mixture. Using your hands, crumble this mixture over the jam.

Bake for 30 to 35 minutes, or until the top is golden brown. Let the bars cool completely in the baking dish. Remove the bars using the parchment handles. Slice into squares.

YOGA COOKIES GF V

These seem like the kind of cookies that just about everyone could eat and enjoy! I like to gobble one down when I come out of Saturday morning yoga and I'm feeling ready to tackle chores and play. The cookies are on the healthier side as far as cookies go—relying on peanut butter and vegan butter for creaminess, and oats and gluten-free flour for structure. They've also got nutritious add-ins: cranberries, pumpkin seeds, walnuts and cinnamon. They're not just good for you, they're also delicious. If you're baking for health-conscious friends who are vegan and/or gluten-free, they'll love these, but so will friends who have no such concerns and simply want something delicious.

Makes 20–24 cookies

½ cup (114 g) best quality vegan butter, softened

1 cup (200 g) granulated sugar

1½ tbsp (30 g) molasses

½ cup (129 g) creamy peanut butter, not natural style

1 tsp vanilla extract

1 tsp cinnamon

½ tsp salt

1 tsp baking powder

½ tsp baking soda

1 cup (90 g) quick-cooking gluten-free oats

¾ cup (94 g) gluten-free flour blend (you can use all-purpose flour if you aren't concerned about gluten)

½ cup (60 g) dried cranberries, coarsely chopped

½ cup (69 g) pepitas (shelled pumpkin seeds)

½ cup (59 g) walnuts, toasted

Preheat the oven to 350°F (175°C). Line two baking sheets with parchment paper and spray with cooking spray.

In a large bowl, using a wooden spoon, cream together the butter, sugar and molasses until light and fluffy, about 2 minutes. Stir in the peanut butter and vanilla. Add the cinnamon, salt, baking powder and baking soda, stirring until well combined. Gently stir in the oats, followed by the flour. Add the cranberries, pepitas and walnuts. Roll the cookie dough into 2-inch (5-cm) balls.

Place the balls on the cookie sheets with 2 inches (5 cm) of space between them. Flatten slightly with your fingers. Bake the cookies for 10 to 12 minutes, or until the cookies are crinkled and puffed. Remove from the oven and let cool for 10 minutes before removing to a rack to cool completely. Store in an airtight container for up to a week.

NO-BAKE WHITE VANILLA PEANUT BUTTER COOKIES (GF)

We all love the traditional chocolate and peanut butter no-bake cookies, but I wanted to create a different version of the recipe for the people in my family that prefer white chocolate. The chocolate eschewers have been missing out on lots of cookies and treats, so with them in mind, I created these no-bake cookies. And for those that don't even like white chocolate, these cookies are technically not even white chocolate since I created the recipe with vanilla candy coating, which is more stable and easier to work with than white chocolate. It took me several attempts to get the recipe just right, but now these have become a family favorite. They run on the sweet side, so if you don't want to add the salted peanuts, you may want to finish the cookies with a sprinkle of sea salt.

Makes 24 cookies

½ cup (120 ml) milk

2 cups (400 g) granulated sugar

16 oz (454 g) vanilla candy coating

½ cup (114 g) unsalted butter

½ tsp salt

2 tsp (10 ml) vanilla extract

½ cup (129 g) creamy peanut butter, not natural style

3¼ cups (293 g) quick-cooking gluten-free oats

¾ cup (110 g) chopped salted peanuts

Lay out a large sheet of waxed paper on a flat surface.

In a medium saucepan, heat the milk, sugar, candy coating, butter and salt over medium heat. Stir constantly until the mixture comes to a full boil. Remove from the heat. Stir in the vanilla and peanut butter, mixing until smooth. Quickly fold in the oats and peanuts while the mixture is still hot. Drop 2 tablespoons (28 g) of the oat mixture at a time onto the waxed paper. Let cool completely before serving.

CHOCOLATE, BUTTERSCOTCH
AND PEANUT BUTTER SCOTCHEROOS

I had never tasted a Scotcheroo, or Scotch-a-Woo, as my nephew Reeve who couldn't say his *R*s used to call them, until I moved to Utah a few years ago. I don't know why the whole world doesn't know about them yet. Scotcheroos are essentially a sweet peanut butter cereal bar with a chocolate and butterscotch topping. My variation uses double the normal amount of chocolate and butterscotch for a topping that's almost as thick as the cereal bar itself. Yes, you're welcome for that. If you need a treat for a bake sale or a tailgating party, these are as fast to make and easy to transport as a rice cereal treat, but they're extra wonderful. Ladies and gentlemen, I give you Scotch-a-Woos!

Makes 16 bars

BARS

1 cup (240 ml) light corn syrup

1 cup (200 g) granulated sugar

1 cup (258 g) creamy peanut butter, not natural style

1 tsp vanilla extract

6 cups (128 g) crispy rice cereal

TOPPING

2 cups (336 g) semisweet chocolate chips

2 cups (336 g) butterscotch chips

Coat a 9 x 13–inch (23 x 33–cm) baking dish with cooking spray.

To make the bars, in a large pot over medium heat, place the corn syrup and granulated sugar. Cook, stirring constantly, until the sugar dissolves and the mixture begins to boil. Remove from the heat and add the peanut butter and vanilla. Stir until the mixture is smooth, then add the rice cereal. Carefully pour the mixture into the prepared baking dish. Wet your hands slightly and gently press the mixture into the pan to even it out.

Make the topping by melting the chocolate chips and butterscotch chips in a medium saucepan over low heat. When the chips have melted, stir the mixture until very smooth and glossy. Pour the mixture over the prepared bars.

Let the bars rest until the topping is firm, then cut into bars. The bars will stay fresh, if stored in an airtight container, for 1 week.

NEW ORLEANS PECAN PRALINE COOKIES

I went on a work trip to New Orleans a few years ago, but if you would have spied on me, you would have thought I was only there to eat. Don't ever go to New Orleans on a diet, OK? Promise? It's important. If you ever want to eat your way through a city, go to NOLA, and get yourself a big bag of pecan pralines. Maybe buy an extra bag to take home, too. Trust me. Pralines are a confection that have a rich, nutty flavor from lots of brown sugar and pecans. These cookies are my riff on New Orleans's signature candy, with their pronounced brown sugar flavor and melt-in-your-mouth topping that is full of toasted pecans.

Makes 24 cookies

COOKIES

11 tbsp (154 g) unsalted butter, softened

1½ cups (330 g) dark brown sugar, packed

1 egg

1 tsp vanilla extract

½ tsp salt

½ tsp baking powder

1½ tsp (7 g) baking soda

2 cups (250 g) all-purpose flour

TOPPING

⅔ cup (160 ml) heavy whipping cream

½ cup (110 g) dark brown sugar, packed

Generous pinch of salt

2 cups (240 g) powdered sugar

¾ cup (82 g) chopped pecans, toasted, plus more for the tops of the cookies

Preheat the oven to 350°F (175°C). Line two baking sheets with parchment paper.

To make the cookies, in a large bowl, cream together the butter and sugar until light and fluffy. Add the egg and vanilla. Sprinkle the salt, baking powder and baking soda over the dough. Stir for 1 minute. Gently stir in the flour. Make 24 dough balls using about 1½ tablespoons (21 g) of dough each. Place on the prepared cookie sheets about 2 inches (5 cm) apart. Bake for 8 to 10 minutes, or until the tops are just set and the edges are just beginning to brown. Don't overbake. Cool the cookies for 5 minutes on the cookie sheets and then transfer to a rack to cool completely.

While the cookies cool, prepare the topping. In a medium saucepan over medium heat, bring the cream and brown sugar to a boil, stirring constantly for exactly 2 minutes. Remove from the heat and stir in the salt. Let the mixture cool for about 10 minutes, then stir in the powdered sugar and fold in the pecans. The mixture should be loose enough to spoon over the cookies, but if it isn't, just put it over the heat again. It can be warmed back up at any point. Spoon the filling over the cookies and sprinkle with additional pecans.

WHITE CHOCOLATE
CADBURY EGG COOKIES

A couple of years ago we went through a Cadbury Mini Egg obsession at our house.
When the Easter season was over we were all sad that they were gone. Then I spotted a few bags
in the sale section of the drugstore, so I brought home two bags, one for Sailor and one for West.
West was smart and hid his in the mini fridge in his room, but Sailor left hers in the cupboard.
After a couple of weeks, I had eaten the whole bag and Sailor didn't get any. Luckily I was able
to buy her another bag before she could mourn the loss. Now you can find Cadbury Mini Eggs
for sale almost any time of year, but always in seasonally appropriate colors.
Great—now I can make these cookies whenever I want!

Makes 12 very large cookies

½ cup (114 g) unsalted butter, softened

⅓ cup (66 g) granulated sugar

⅔ cup plus 1 tbsp (161 g) brown sugar, packed

1 egg

1½ tsp (8 ml) vanilla extract

½ tsp salt

¾ tsp baking powder

½ tsp baking soda

1½ cups (188 g) all-purpose flour

¾ cup (138 g) candy-coated milk chocolate miniature eggs, plus more for poking into the tops (I recommend Cadbury Mini Eggs [not Cadbury Crème Eggs])

⅓ cup (55 g) white chocolate chips, plus more for poking into the tops

⅓ cup (55 g) milk chocolate chips

Preheat the oven to 350°F (175°C). Line two baking sheets with parchment paper.

In a large bowl, beat the butter, granulated sugar and brown sugar until light and fluffy. Add the egg and vanilla. Sprinkle the salt, baking powder and baking soda over the dough and mix well. Gently stir in the flour. Add the mini eggs, white chocolate chips and milk chocolate chips.

Divide the dough into 12 equal portions and roll them into balls. Evenly distribute the balls on the two cookie sheets and bake for about 10 to 12 minutes, or until just showing signs of browning on top. Do not overbake. Immediately poke more miniature eggs and white chocolate chips into the tops of the cookies. The cookies will continue to set on the baking sheets. Allow them to rest until they are completely cooled.

ALMOND SAND DOLLARS

I started making cookies by myself when I was fairly young. My mom, to her credit, never made me wait and ask permission. She never made me feel like I was using up an ingredient that she had planned for later. She never acted annoyed when I made a bad batch or left a mess in the kitchen. This is a gift for an aspiring baker. I don't think it's a coincidence that every one of my siblings—all seven sisters and both brothers—are proficient cookie bakers. Some of us love baking more than others, but all of us can turn out a batch of beautiful and delicious cookies. Thank you for that, Mom.

This is one of the first cookies that I learned to make myself. In my young mind, these were the height of elegance, beauty and cleverness. I guess I still think that! The cookies look just like a little sand dollar you would find on the beach. The flavor is predominantly almond, but if you prefer vanilla, you could use that instead. The almond flavor does play so nicely with the cookie design.

Makes about 30 cookies

COOKIES

½ cup (114 g) unsalted butter, softened

¼ cup plus 2 tbsp (80 g) granulated sugar, plus more for flattening the cookies

½ tsp almond extract

½ tsp vanilla extract

¼ tsp salt

¼ tsp baking powder

1 cup (125 g) all-purpose flour

GLAZE

1 cup (120 g) powdered sugar

1 tbsp (15 ml) milk or water

1½ tsp (8 ml) almond extract

Sliced almonds, for the tops

Preheat the oven to 400°F (205°C). Line two baking sheets with parchment paper.

To make the cookies, cream the butter and sugar until light and fluffy. Add the almond extract and vanilla. Sprinkle the salt and baking powder over the dough. Mix well. Gently stir in the flour. Roll the dough into 1-inch (2.5-cm) balls and place on the prepared baking sheets about 2 inches (5 cm) apart. Use the bottom of a drinking glass dipped in granulated sugar to flatten the cookies. Bake the cookies for about 7 to 8 minutes, or until the edges are just beginning to brown. Let the cookies cool for 5 minutes on the baking sheets before transferring to a rack to cool completely.

Prepare the glaze by combining the powdered sugar, milk and almond extract. Spoon the glaze over the cookies and press a few almonds onto the top in a sand dollar design.

CHERRY CHEESECAKE BARS

Even though I know little George Washington probably didn't chop down
that cherry tree, the story has become part of American legend. It's a good lesson on telling the
truth, but I like the story even better because it makes me feel like I can serve a cherry dessert
in the name of patriotic pride on George's birthday—though I do make these cherry bars more
often than that. If you need something special and unique for a bake sale when you know
everyone else is bringing chocolate chip cookies and rice cereal bars, pack up this pretty treat
and watch it turn into a bestseller. There are a lot of layers to this beautiful bar,
but I keep it manageable by using only one bowl for prep.

Makes 18 bars

CRUST AND TOPPING

½ cup (114 g) unsalted butter, softened

1¼ cups (250 g) granulated sugar

¼ tsp salt

2 cups (250 g) all-purpose flour

FILLING

2 (8-oz [226-g]) blocks of cream cheese, softened

2 tsp (10 ml) vanilla extract

1 egg

½ cup (100 g) granulated sugar

2 tbsp (16 g) all-purpose flour

1 (21-oz [594-g]) can cherry pie filling, roughly mashed with a fork to burst any whole berries

Preheat the oven to 350°F (175°C). Line a 9 x 13–inch (23 x 33–cm) baking dish with parchment paper, cut to fit the bottom, with enough extra to hang over the edges to create handles to pull out the bars when they are finished baking. Lightly coat the parchment paper with cooking spray.

To make the crust and topping, in a large bowl, combine the butter, sugar, salt and flour, mixing until crumbly. Reserve 1¼ cups (280 g) of the crumb mixture and press the remaining mixture into the bottom of the prepared baking dish. Bake for 10 minutes.

Meanwhile, prepare the filling. Wipe out the large bowl with a paper towel and add in the cream cheese, vanilla and egg, beating until creamy and well combined. Stir in the sugar and flour.

Spoon the cream cheese filling over the hot crust when it comes out of the oven, spreading the filling to the edges. Pour the cherry pie filling over the cream cheese mixture. Crumble the reserved crumb mixture over the cherries and return the bars to the oven. Bake for 40 to 50 minutes, or until the bars are bubbling on the edges and the topping is golden brown. Place the pan on a rack to cool completely. Remove the bars from the pan and cut into squares. Store in the fridge for up to 1 week.

CREAM CHEESE SHORTBREAD HALF-DIPPED HEARTS

These elegant, heart-shaped shortbread cookies are one of my favorites for Valentine's Day. I'm happy to make them any day, and if it's not Valentine's Day, I'll cut them into squares and dip the chocolate on the diagonal, or I'll cut them into circles instead of hearts. If you don't want to dip the shortbread into chocolate, you could sprinkle a little bit of coarse sugar on top before baking. I love mine with the chocolate coating, but I do always eat the plain side first and save the chocolaty (best) side for last.

Makes about 36 cookies

1 cup (227 g) unsalted butter, softened

3 oz (86 g) cream cheese, softened

1 cup (200 g) granulated sugar

1½ tsp (8 ml) vanilla extract

¼ tsp salt

2 egg yolks

2½ cups (313 g) all-purpose flour, plus more for the work surface

Cold water, if needed

12 oz (340 g) dark chocolate candy coating

Decorative sprinkles, optional

In a medium bowl, using an electric mixer, beat the butter, cream cheese and sugar until creamy. This should take a couple of minutes. Add the vanilla and mix until smooth. Add the salt and egg yolks and mix well. Gently stir in the flour. Gather the dough into a ball. If the dough is too dry, sprinkle with a little cold water before gathering. Wrap the dough tightly in plastic wrap and chill in the fridge for 2 hours, or up to 1 week.

Preheat the oven to 375°F (190°C). Line two baking sheets with parchment paper.

Roll the dough out on a floured surface to ¼-inch (6-mm) thickness. Using a 3-inch (7.5-cm) heart-shaped cookie cutter, cut hearts from the dough and place on the baking sheets with an inch (2.5 cm) of space between them. Bake for 7 to 9 minutes, watching closely, until the cookies are just golden brown on the edges.

Let the cookies cool completely on the cookie sheet. Meanwhile, in a medium microwaveable bowl, heat the candy coating on 50 percent power for 1 minute. Remove from the microwave and stir. Continue to microwave and stir in 30-second intervals until the chocolate is completely melted and smooth. Dip the cooled shortbread hearts in the chocolate to coat just one side. If you like, add sprinkles to the chocolate side. Let the chocolate cool until completely set before serving, about 1 hour.

CARROT CAKE WHOOPIE PIES WITH CINNAMON CREAM CHEESE FILLING

These carrot cake whoopie pies are a fun twist on a traditional carrot cake, but I like them even better since they're made with butter instead of oil like traditional carrot cake. I also always appreciate a treat that can be eaten straight from the hand, no spoon or fork required.

Makes about 15 sandwich cookies

COOKIES

½ cup (114 g) unsalted butter, softened

½ cup (100 g) granulated sugar

½ cup (110 g) brown sugar, packed

2 eggs

1 tsp vanilla extract

1 tsp cinnamon

½ tsp ginger

¼ tsp nutmeg

½ tsp salt

1½ tsp (7 g) baking powder

1¼ (6 g) tsp baking soda

2 cups (250 g) all-purpose flour

1½ cups (165 g) finely grated raw carrot

1 cup (109 g) chopped pecans

FILLING

½ cup (114 g) unsalted butter, softened

1 (8-oz [226-g]) block of cream cheese, room temperature

1 tsp vanilla extract

Generous pinch of salt

1 tsp cinnamon

3 cups (360 g) powdered sugar, plus more if needed

Preheat the oven to 350°F (175°C). Line two baking sheets with parchment paper.

To prepare the cookies, in a large bowl, using an electric mixer, cream together the butter, granulated sugar and brown sugar until light and fluffy. Add the eggs and vanilla. Sprinkle the cinnamon, ginger, nutmeg, salt, baking powder and baking soda over the dough. Stir vigorously for 1 minute. Gently stir in the flour. Fold in the carrot and pecans. Measure ¼ cup (56 g) of the dough at a time and drop onto the prepared baking sheets.

Bake for 12 to 14 minutes, or until puffed and golden brown. Let the cookies cool for 5 minutes on the baking sheets before transferring to a rack to cool completely.

Make the filling by beating the butter, cream cheese and vanilla in a large bowl until light and fluffy. Sprinkle in the salt and cinnamon and beat for 1 minute. Add the powdered sugar, a little at a time, to form a thick and fluffy filling.

Frost the bottom of one cookie generously and then top with an unfrosted cookie, forming a sandwich. Press the cookies together so that frosting oozes out of the edges a bit.

HAPPY BIRTHDAY CAKE BATTER COOKIES

Birthday cake batter has become a huge flavor sensation, but if you ask around,
most people aren't sure what the flavor even is. What is the flavor of birthday cake batter?
If it's vanilla and egg, those are part of the flavor profile of most baked goods. I think birthday
cake flavor should have a richness from egg yolks, and a touch of perfumed sweetness from both
vanilla and almond extracts. The easiest way to get this flavor is to use cake batter extract,
but if you can't find it, use 1 teaspoon each of vanilla and almond extracts in the cookies,
and a ½ teaspoon each of vanilla and almond extracts in the frosting.

Makes 24 cookies

COOKIES

¾ cup (170 g) unsalted butter, softened

1½ cups (300 g) granulated sugar

3 egg yolks

2 tsp (10 ml) cake batter extract

½ tsp salt

½ tsp baking soda

2¾ cups (344 g) all-purpose flour, plus more if needed

1 cup (288 g) rainbow sprinkles, plus more for the tops of the cookies

FROSTING

3 tbsp (42 g) unsalted butter, softened

Pinch of salt

4 cups (480 g) powdered sugar, plus more if needed

3 tbsp (45 ml) milk

1 tsp cake batter extract

Preheat the oven to 350°F (175°C). Line two baking sheets with parchment paper.

To make the cookies, in a large bowl, beat together the butter and sugar until light and creamy. Stir in the egg yolks and cake batter extract. Sprinkle the salt and baking soda over the dough and mix well. Gently stir in the flour. The dough should be slightly sticky. If the dough is very sticky, add more flour a tablespoon (15 g) at a time. Fold in the sprinkles. Shape the dough into 2-inch (5-cm) balls and place on the prepared baking sheets at least 2 inches (5 cm) apart. Using the bottom of a drinking glass, gently flatten the cookies.

Bake for 8 to 10 minutes, or until just beginning to brown. Let the cookies cool on the baking sheets for 10 minutes before removing to a rack and cooling completely.

Prepare the frosting by combining the butter, salt and 1 cup (120 g) of sugar. Add the milk and cake batter extract. Stir in the remaining sugar and beat the frosting until light and fluffy, adding more powdered sugar if needed. Frost the cooled cookies generously and sprinkle with additional sprinkles.

DUTCH SPICE COOKIES

I've been making these Dutch spice cookies since Sailor and West were teeny-tiny. At Christmastime, we like to celebrate the Dutch tradition of Santa Claus. Sailor and West leave their shoes by the fireplace, and "Sinter Klaas" fills their shoes with candy and these Dutch cookies that I bake the night before. It's also a tradition to get new shoes this night, since I don't like the idea of leaving candy and cookies by used shoes. Ha!

You'll recognize the warm, comforting flavors in these cookies from cookie butter, which has become so popular in the United States. In fact, if you want to make a little cookie butter, just crumble a few of these cookies and puree them with a little butter and condensed milk to form a peanut butter–like consistency. There you go—cookie butter!

Makes 40 cookies

½ cup (114 g) unsalted butter, softened

1 cup (220 g) brown sugar, packed

1 egg

¼ tsp salt

¾ tsp baking powder

¼ tsp baking soda

1 tsp cinnamon

1 tsp ginger

1 tsp allspice

½ tsp cloves

½ tsp nutmeg

1½ cups (313 g) all-purpose flour, plus more for the work surface

In a large bowl, mix the butter and sugar until light and creamy, about 2 minutes. Add the egg and stir to combine. Sprinkle the salt, baking powder, baking soda, cinnamon, ginger, allspice, cloves and nutmeg over the batter. Mix for 2 minutes, or until all the spices and powders are thoroughly combined. Gently stir in the flour. Gather the dough into a ball and wrap in plastic wrap. Chill the dough for at least 2 hours, or up to 1 week. About 15 minutes before you are ready to bake, take the cookie dough out and leave it on the counter.

Preheat the oven to 350°F (175°C). Line two baking sheets with parchment paper.

Lightly flour a work surface. Roll the dough to a thickness of ¼ to ½ inch (6 to 13 mm). You can use a special Dutch cookie cutter, but I like to cut the cookies into rectangles. Simple! Bake the cookies on the prepared cookie sheets, leaving about 1 inch (3 cm) of space between cookies, for about 12 to 15 minutes, or until starting to brown on the edges.

HAWAIIAN SNOWBALLS

My little sister Heidi used to tease me because I didn't like coconut. Every time I would say I didn't like it, Heidi would quote the movie *It's a Wonderful Life* when little Donna Reid tells Jimmy Stewart that she doesn't like coconut: "Say, brainless, don't you know where coconuts come from?" My sister doesn't have to tease me anymore because I've turned into a coconut lover as an adult. Now she has other things to tease me about. Heidi shouldn't tease me too much anyway, because then she won't get these buttery little cookies that pack a huge hit of coconut from both the coconut extract and the sweetened, shredded coconut.

Makes 24 cookies

½ cup (114 g) unsalted butter, softened

¾ cup (90 g) powdered sugar, divided

1 tsp coconut extract

1 cup (125 g) all-purpose flour

¼ tsp salt

1 cup (62 g) sweetened shredded coconut, coarsely chopped

Preheat the oven to 350°F (175°C). Line a baking sheet with parchment paper.

In a large bowl, using a wooden spoon, beat the butter and ¼ cup (30 g) of powdered sugar until light and creamy. Stir in the coconut extract. Add the flour and salt, stirring until just combined. Fold in the coconut.

Roll the cookies into 1-inch (2.5-cm) balls and arrange evenly on the baking sheet with about 2 inches (5 cm) of space between them. Bake for about 10 minutes, or until just beginning to brown. Let the cookies cool for 4 minutes and then transfer to a rack.

Place the remaining powdered sugar into a bowl. Roll the warm cookies, one at a time, in the sugar. Let the cookies cool completely before serving.

VERMONT MAPLE
WHITE CHOCOLATE COOKIES

I never miss an autumn in New England if I can help it. One year when we were on an October leaf-peeping trip to Vermont, we splurged on a maple-themed lunch at a small cafe, including a top-notch grilled cheese sandwich with smoky ham, apples and maple mustard, a maple–butternut squash soup and a fabulous white chocolate and pecan maple cookie with a rich glaze. I had to come home and re-create that memorable cookie—and the rest of that meal, too, but that is for another cookbook on another day.

Makes 24 cookies

COOKIES

1 cup (109 g) chopped pecans, divided

½ cup (114 g) unsalted butter, melted and cooled slightly

¼ cup (50 g) granulated sugar

½ cup (110 g) brown sugar, packed

1 egg

2 tsp (10 ml) maple extract

½ tsp salt

½ tsp baking powder

½ tsp baking soda

1½ cups (188 g) all-purpose flour

¾ cup (126 g) white chocolate chips

GLAZE

3 tbsp (42 g) unsalted butter

1 cup (120 g) powdered sugar

3 tbsp (45 ml) pure maple syrup (I like grade B for the strongest flavor)

¼ tsp maple extract

Preheat the oven to 350°F (175°C). Line two baking sheets with parchment paper.

To toast the pecans, place on a rimmed cookie sheet, and bake at 350°F (175°C) for 7 to 9 minutes, stirring occasionally, until the pecans are fragrant and take on a deeper shade of brown.

To prepare the cookies, in a large bowl, cream the butter, granulated sugar and brown sugar until light and fluffy. Add the egg and maple extract. Sprinkle the salt, baking powder and baking soda over the dough, and mix well. Gently stir in the flour. Stir in ¾ cup (82 g) of the pecans and the white chocolate chips.

Shape the dough into ping-pong-sized balls. Place on the prepared baking sheets about 2 inches (5 cm) apart. Bake the cookies for about 7 to 9 minutes, or until just set on top. Immediately poke the remaining pecans into the tops of the cookies. Let the cookies rest on the baking sheets for 5 minutes and then transfer to a rack to cool completely.

To prepare the glaze, melt the butter in a medium saucepan over low heat. Add the powdered sugar, maple syrup and maple extract. Stir until a smooth glaze forms. Drizzle the glaze over the cooled cookies. Let the glaze set before serving.

CLASSIC SNICKERDOODLES

If I'm baking for lots of kids, these are the best bet cookies in my repertoire. I've yet to meet a child—or adult, come to think of it—that wouldn't cozy up to a snickerdoodle. A classic snickerdoodle should have both butter and shortening so it can be flavorful, crinkly and chewy with crisp edges. But kids won't care about that explanation. They'll only care that snickerdoodles are warm and comforting and yummy. Here's my go-to kid's lunch menu when my nieces and nephews are visiting: grilled cheese sandwiches, mini pretzels, apple slices and these snickerdoodles, warm from the oven.

Makes about 18 cookies

¼ cup (57 g) unsalted butter, softened

¼ cup (48 g) vegetable shortening, softened

1¼ cups (250 g) granulated sugar, divided

1 egg

1 tsp vanilla extract

¼ tsp salt

¼ tsp cream of tartar

¼ tsp baking soda

1½ cups (188 g) all-purpose flour

1 tbsp (8 g) cinnamon

Preheat the oven to 375°F (190°C). Line two baking sheets with parchment paper.

In a large bowl, cream together the butter, shortening and 1 cup (200 g) of granulated sugar. Add the egg and vanilla. Sprinkle the salt, cream of tartar and baking soda over the dough. Stir for 1 minute. Add the flour and stir until just combined. Roll the dough into 1-inch (2.5-cm) balls. In a small bowl, combine the remaining granulated sugar and cinnamon. Roll each ball generously in the cinnamon-sugar mixture and place on the prepared baking sheets.

Bake for 9 to 11 minutes. If you like them soft and chewy, stick to 9 minutes, but if you like them crisp on the outer edges, bake for the full 11 minutes.

CAMPFIRE SURPRISE COOKIES

When you're craving s'mores, but you're not in the woods, make these three-layer cookies. The cookies have an appealing sandy texture from ground graham cracker crumbs, topped with a layer of toasted marshmallow and a rich chocolate frosting. The best bites have generous amounts of marshmallow, so keep the cookies on the smaller side so there is marshmallow in every delicious bite.

Makes about 30 cookies

COOKIES

½ cup (114 g) unsalted butter, softened

¾ cup (165 g) brown sugar, packed

1 egg

1 tsp vanilla extract

¼ tsp salt

¾ tsp baking powder

½ tsp baking soda

1½ cups (135 g) graham cracker crumbs (made from 9 full graham cracker sheets pulsed in the blender or food processor)

¾ cup (94 g) all-purpose flour

15 large marshmallows, cut in half

FROSTING

2 tbsp (28 g) unsalted butter, softened

2 tbsp (11 g) cocoa powder

1 tbsp (15 ml) milk, plus more if needed

1 cup (120 g) powdered sugar, plus more if needed

Preheat the oven to 350°F (175°C). Line two baking sheets with parchment paper.

To make the cookies, in a large bowl, mix the butter and the sugar until light and fluffy. Sir in the egg and vanilla. Sprinkle the salt, baking powder and baking soda over the top. Gently stir in the graham cracker crumbs and the flour. Roll the cookies into 1-inch (2.5-cm) balls.

Bake for 5 minutes and remove from the oven. Press a marshmallow piece in the top of the cookie, being very careful not to touch the hot pan. Return the cookies to the oven and bake until the marshmallows begin to turn golden brown, about 4 to 6 minutes. Remove from the oven. Let the cookies cool for 5 minutes on the baking sheets before transferring to a rack to cool completely.

Prepare the frosting by melting the butter in a medium saucepan over low heat. Whisk in the cocoa powder and then the milk. Remove from the heat and stir in the powdered sugar. Add more milk or powdered sugar as needed until the frosting is a loose, spreadable consistency.

Spread the frosting over the warm cookies, covering just the marshmallow. I like to leave just a sliver of marshmallow unfrosted so you can see what you're getting under there.

PATRIOTIC M&M COOKIES

One July I walked into my sister Lisa's house ready to babysit her girls while she and her husband went away for a few days to celebrate their anniversary. It turned out to be the best gig, because not only were there a bunch of freshly bathed, cute nieces in curlers and nightgowns to spend the summer weekend with, but also because my sister had baked M&M cookies for us to enjoy. I've made these cookies every July since then, and I always think of that happy summer night.

P.S. Don't wait until July to make these. Just change the M&M colors and you could make these for any holiday—or any regular day.

Makes about 36 cookies

1 cup (227 g) unsalted butter, softened

1 cup (220 g) brown sugar, packed (I prefer dark, but light also works)

¾ cup (150 g) granulated sugar

2 eggs, room temperature

1 tbsp (15 ml) vanilla extract

1 tsp salt

1 tsp baking powder

1 tsp baking soda

3 cups (375 g) all-purpose flour

1 (11-oz [311-g]) bag red and blue candy-coated chocolates, divided (I recommend M&M's)

1 cup (168 g) white chocolate chips, divided

Preheat the oven to 350°F (175°C). Line a baking sheet with parchment paper.

In a large mixing bowl, with a wooden spoon or mixer, combine the butter, brown sugar and granulated sugar until light and fluffy. Add the eggs and vanilla, stirring until well combined. Sprinkle the salt, baking powder and baking soda over the top of the butter mixture and mix well. If you're using a mixer, stop and switch to a wooden spoon. Add the flour, 1 cup (125 g) at a time, mixing gently until well blended. Stir in half of the candy-coated chocolates and half of the chocolate chips. Shape the dough into generous 1-inch (2.5-cm) balls and place on the prepared baking sheet. Bake the cookies for 7 to 9 minutes, or until puffed and just beginning to brown on the edges. The centers should still be slightly underdone.

Remove the cookies from the oven. Immediately press a few candy-coated chocolates and chocolate chips into the top of each cookie, tucking them in a bit so that they will stay put. Let the cookies cool on the baking sheet for about 10 minutes, then transfer to a rack to cool completely.

NEW-FASHIONED SEA SALT AND BROWNED BUTTER CHOCOLATE CHUNK COOKIES WITH CHOCOLATE-COVERED ALMONDS

I never met a chocolate chip cookie that I didn't like. Wait, let me clarify. I never met a homemade chocolate chip cookie that I didn't like, although some are better than others, aren't they? This is one of my favorite versions. It's full of modern ingredients, like browned butter, sea salt and dark chocolate, but it still feels old fashioned and familiar, since it's still at its essence a chocolate chip cookie. It's like a chocolate chip cookie that grew up in the country, moved to the city and had a fancy career, then decided it liked the countryside better and moved back home.

P.S. To be a "New-Fashioned" cookie, it should have dark chocolate almonds and dark chocolate chunks, but I often make the cookie with semisweet chunks and milk chocolate almonds because my kids have not yet warmed up to dark chocolate. It's fantastic, no matter what.

Makes 12 big cookies

1 cup (227 g) unsalted butter

1⅓ cups (293 g) dark brown sugar, packed

⅓ cup (66 g) granulated sugar

2 eggs plus 1 egg yolk

1 tbsp (15 ml) vanilla extract

1 tsp sea salt

1 tsp baking powder

1 tsp baking soda

2½ cups (313 g) all-purpose flour

1¾ cups (322 g) dark or milk chocolate–covered almonds, coarsely chopped, plus more for the tops

1 cup (168 g) dark or semisweet chocolate discs or chunks

Flaked sea salt, for the tops (I recommend Maldon)

In a medium saucepan over medium heat, melt the butter and bring to a simmer. Swirl the pan and watch for the butter to change color to light brown. When you start to see brown flecks at the bottom of the pan, remove the pan from the heat. Transfer the browned butter to a large bowl and let it cool for 30 minutes.

Add the brown sugar and granulated sugar to the cooled butter and beat until fluffy, about 4 minutes. Add the eggs and egg yolk and vanilla. Sprinkle the sea salt, baking powder and baking soda over the dough. Stir well. Add the flour, mixing very gently to combine. Fold in the almonds and chocolate discs. Cover the dough with plastic wrap and let it rest for 20 minutes. Shape the dough into 12 separate balls and place in a zip-top bag. Refrigerate for at least 24 hours, or up to 5 days.

When ready to bake, preheat the oven to 375°F (190°C). Line two baking sheets with parchment paper.

Bake the cookies for 9 to 12 minutes, or until the cookies start to turn golden brown on top. Immediately pick up one baking pan at a time with a hot pad, hold the pan about 1 foot (30 cm) above the counter, and drop the baking sheet onto the counter. Do this a couple of times until the cookies flatten out a bit. Sprinkle the tops of the cookies with the flaked sea salt and poke in a few chocolate-covered almonds. Let cool for 10 minutes before removing to a rack to cool completely.

CHOCOLATE WHOOPIE PIES

My best college friend Kimmarie likes to lay claim to whoopie pies as a Pennsylvania-invented treat. She's a Philly girl herself. I'm not sure where they came from, but it was definitely somewhere back east. Sources say it was either Maine, Massachusetts, New Hampshire or Pennsylvania. I love chocolate whoopie pies with cream cheese frosting and candy canes at Christmas, with chocolate and nuts for a decadent treat or with peanut butter frosting and pretzels to satisfy my need for sweet and salty. Use any variation to make them your own—but definitely make them!

Makes about 30 sandwich cookies

COOKIES
½ cup (114 g) unsalted butter, softened

¾ cup (165 g) brown sugar, packed

¼ cup (50 g) granulated sugar

1 egg

1½ tsp (8 ml) vanilla extract

½ cup (44 g) cocoa powder

½ tsp salt

1½ tsp (7 g) baking soda

1 cup (240 ml) milk or buttermilk

2 cups (250 g) all-purpose flour

CHOCOLATE PEPPERMINT FROSTING
½ cup (114 g) unsalted butter, softened

1 tsp peppermint extract

½ tsp vanilla extract

Pinch of salt

1 tbsp (15 ml) milk, plus more if needed

4 cups (480 g) powdered sugar

1 cup (232 g) crushed candy canes or sprinkles, for the edges

CHOCOLATE WALNUT FROSTING
¼ cup (22 g) cocoa powder

½ tsp espresso powder, optional

½ cup (114 g) unsalted butter, softened

1 tbsp (15 ml) milk, plus more if needed

4 cups (480 g) powdered sugar

1 cup (117 g) chopped walnuts, for the edges

PEANUT BUTTER PRETZEL FROSTING
2 cups (192 g) marshmallow fluff

½ cup (129 g) creamy peanut butter

1 tbsp (15 ml) milk, plus more if needed

⅛ tsp salt

1 tsp vanilla extract

4 cups (480 g) powdered sugar

1 cup (40 g) crushed pretzels, for the edges

Preheat the oven to 350°F (175°C). Line two baking sheets with parchment paper.

To make the cookies, in a large bowl, cream together the butter, brown sugar and granulated sugar until light and fluffy. Add the egg and vanilla. Sprinkle the cocoa powder, salt and baking soda over the batter. Mix well. Add the milk and stir until combined. The mixture might appear to separate, but it will come back together. Gently stir in the flour. The dough will be sticky.

Drop the dough by tablespoonfuls (14 g) onto the prepared cookie sheets, about 2 inches (5 cm) apart. Bake until set and puffed, about 10 minutes. Let cool completely on the baking sheets.

Prepare the frosting of your choice from the variations above. Beat all of the frosting ingredients, until the last ingredient, together for whichever variation you choose. The frosting should be very thick. Frost the bottom of one cookie generously and then top with an unfrosted cookie, forming a sandwich. Press the cookies together so that frosting oozes out the edges a bit. Roll the edges of the cookies into the corresponding last ingredient listed in the variation that you have chosen.

NANTUCKET CRANBERRY, ORANGE AND WHITE CHOCOLATE OATMEAL COOKIES

If you've ever visited the "Little Grey Lady of the Sea," otherwise known as the island of Nantucket, then you know that it is famous for its cranberries. My husband Shane's family vacationed on Nantucket every year when he was growing up. I grew up in the West and I had never even heard of it until Shane took me there as part of our honeymoon. Nantucket is charm and grace personified. We don't get to Nantucket too often these days, but I can, and often do, replicate the little cranberry white chocolate cookies that we purchased repeatedly at a bakery on Orange Street. Here's a little taste of our favorite island for the next generation.

Makes 24 cookies

½ cup (114 g) unsalted butter, softened

1 cup (220 g) dark brown sugar, packed

1 egg

1 tsp vanilla extract

1 tbsp (10 g) grated orange zest

½ tsp salt

¾ tsp baking soda

1½ cups (188 g) all-purpose flour

1 cup (90 g) old-fashioned oats

¾ cup (126 g) white chocolate chips, plus more for the tops of the cookies

½ cup (61 g) dried cranberries, sweetened (ideally still chewy and fresh)

½ cup (62 g) natural pistachios, shelled and chopped

Preheat the oven to 350°F (175°C). Line two baking sheets with parchment paper.

In a large bowl, using a wooden spoon, cream together the butter and sugar. Add the egg, vanilla and orange zest. Stir in the salt and baking soda. Very gently add the flour and then the oats. Fold in the chocolate chips, cranberries and pistachios. Roll the dough into generous 1-inch (2.5-cm) balls and bake on the prepared baking sheets for 8 to 10 minutes. Immediately poke more white chocolate chips into the tops. Let the cookies cool for at least 5 minutes before transferring to a rack to cool completely.

MICHELLE'S CUTOUT SUGAR COOKIES

My sister Michelle was born on Christmas Eve. She came home from the hospital in a giant red stocking (that she still has) and naturally grew up to be a veritable Christmas queen. I would be happy just to stand outside in the snow and look through the window into her beautifully decorated home. Not surprisingly, Michelle makes the best Christmas sugar cutout cookies. This is the only cutout sugar cookie recipe I use for any holiday, Christmas included. It's a tradition to make Michelle's recipe every Christmas Eve with my family, as kind of a Happy Birthday to my sister, but also so that we have a plate of the very best and cutest cookies for Santa that night. We like to frost the cookies with delicious buttercream frosting in lots of colors, but if you like to make your cookie decorations flawlessly beautiful, use—less delicious, in my opinion—royal icing.

Makes about 48 cookies

QUICK BUTTERCREAM FROSTING

½ cup (114 g) unsalted butter, softened

2 cups (240 g) powdered sugar

2 tsp (10 ml) vanilla

2 tbsp (30 ml) heavy cream or milk

SUGAR COOKIES

1 cup (227 g) unsalted butter, softened

1½ cups (300 g) granulated sugar

2 eggs

2 tsp (10 ml) vanilla extract

½ tsp salt

1 tsp baking powder

3¾ cups (469 g) all-purpose flour

Preheat the oven to 350°F (175°C). Line three to four baking sheets with parchment paper.

To make the frosting, in a medium bowl, beat the butter, powdered sugar, vanilla and heavy cream until light and fluffy.

To make the cookies, in a large bowl, cream the butter and sugar until light and fluffy. Add the eggs and vanilla. Sprinkle the salt and baking powder over the dough. Mix well. Gently stir in the flour. Divide the dough into fourths.

Work with one-quarter of the dough at a time and store the rest in the fridge, tightly covered with plastic wrap. Roll the dough to about ¼-inch (6-mm) thickness and use cookie cutters to create shapes. Place the cut cookies on the parchment-lined baking sheets. The baking time will vary depending on the size of the shapes you use, but you want the cookies to be lightly golden brown on the edges only, so this usually means a bake time of 7 to 11 minutes. Let the cookies cool on the baking sheets for 10 minutes before gently removing to a rack to cool completely. Be sure the cookies are completely cooled before frosting.

EDIBLE BUTTERY PLAYDOUGH COOKIES FOR KIDS

Calling all parents of young children—this is the recipe for you. Do your kids like to play with their food? Eat raw cookie dough when you're trying to cut out cookies? Roll playdough into snakes and balls? This is the cookie and dough for those kids. Go ahead and let them play with their food here. With this edible buttery playdough, it's not only allowed, it's encouraged.

I like to make a big batch of this dough and tint it with a few different colors. My favorite may be to make orange and green dough for shaping into pumpkin cookies. You can even use a toothpick to draw decorative lines down the pumpkin. The design will stay, as long as you retrace the lines right when the cookies come out of the oven.

Makes a varied amount, depending on the shapes and sizes

1 cup (227 g) unsalted butter, softened

½ cup (100 g) granulated sugar

1 tbsp (15 ml) milk

1 tsp vanilla extract

¼ tsp salt

2¼ cups (281 g) all-purpose flour (heated in a large bowl in the microwave on high for 90 seconds, and then cooled completely, so that the dough is safe to eat raw)

Food coloring (at least 3 or 4 different colors)

Preheat the oven to 325°F (165°C). Line baking sheets with parchment paper.

In a large mixing bowl, cream together the butter and sugar until light and fluffy. Add the milk and vanilla and mix well. Add the salt and flour and stir gently. Separate the dough into desired portions and tint with food coloring. Shape into balls and flatten for pumpkins, or use your imagination to create other shapes and figures. Use toothpicks to etch lines in the raw dough. Retrace the lines immediately when the cookies come out of the oven.

Let the kids play and play. You won't hurt this dough. If you do get cookies that make it to the oven, bake them for 13 to 16 minutes on ungreased cookie sheets, or until the cookies are set when you touch the top centers. Let the cookies cool for 2 minutes, then transfer to a wire rack to cool completely.

BAKE SALE CHOCOLATE-GLAZED PEANUT BUTTER OATMEAL BARS

Warning: These are addicting. This makes a huge batch of bars, and if you don't pay attention, before you know it, you'll have eaten a whole row yourself. My sister Heidi and I were pregnant with our sons West and Reeve at the same time, and we made these just about every week and ate them mostly all by ourselves. We grew those babies on oats and peanut butter. I highly recommend being pregnant at the same time as a hungry sister. It was a fun and happy time that I will never forget, and a time that I always think of when I bite into these bars.

Makes 32 bars

BARS

1 cup (227 g) unsalted butter, softened, plus more for greasing the pan

1 cup (200 g) granulated sugar

1 cup (220 g) brown sugar, packed

⅔ cup (172 g) creamy peanut butter, not natural style

2 eggs

1 tsp vanilla extract

½ tsp salt

1 tsp baking soda

2 cups (250 g) all-purpose flour

2 cups (180 g) quick-cooking oats

TOPPING

¾ cup (194 g) creamy peanut butter

GLAZE

½ cup (114 g) unsalted butter

3 tbsp (45 ml) milk

2 cups (240 g) powdered sugar

2 tbsp (11 g) cocoa powder

Pinch of salt

1 tsp vanilla extract

Preheat the oven to 350°F (175°C). Butter a jelly roll pan.

To make the bars, in a large bowl, cream the butter, granulated sugar and brown sugar until light and fluffy. Add the peanut butter, eggs and vanilla. Sprinkle the salt and baking soda over the dough and mix well. Gently stir in the flour and oats. Press the mixture into the prepared pan. Bake for 15 to 18 minutes, or until just golden brown.

To top, immediately spread with the peanut butter.

Prepare the glaze by combining the butter and the milk in a medium saucepan over medium heat. When the butter is melted, remove from the heat and stir in the powdered sugar, cocoa and salt. Add the vanilla. Spoon the glaze over the peanut butter. Let cool completely before cutting into bars.

OLD-FASHIONED WALNUT COOKIES

This is about the simplest cookie you'll ever make! There are only a handful of basic ingredients and a whole lot of walnuts. Don't even add vanilla here, since you want the toasty walnut flavor to come through loud and clear. Actually, I used to make a few cookies without any walnuts when my kids were little and they were picky about nuts. Thank goodness they've outgrown that! I made these cookies for the first time when we were having family over for a barbecue. I wanted to make a simple dessert of root beer floats with a cookie on the side. These make an excellent root beer and vanilla bean ice cream float partner. One of these days I might even try these cookies with a little bit of root beer extract added into the dough—but on second thought—why mess with perfection?

Makes 36 cookies

1 cup (117 g) chopped walnuts, toasted, plus 36 whole walnuts, untoasted, for the tops

¾ cup (170 g) unsalted butter, softened

¾ cup (165 g) brown sugar, packed

¼ tsp salt

1¼ cups (156 g) all-purpose flour

Preheat the oven to 350°F (175°C). Line two baking sheets with parchment paper.

To toast the chopped walnuts, place on a rimmed cookie sheet, and bake at 350°F (175°C) for 7 to 9 minutes, stirring occasionally, until the walnuts are fragrant and take on a deeper shade of brown.

In a large bowl, beat the butter and sugar until light and fluffy. Mix in the salt and flour, stopping just as soon as the flour is well incorporated. Fold in the chopped walnuts. Roll the cookie dough into 1½-inch (3.75-cm) balls. Using your hands, flatten the cookies to a ½-inch (1.25-cm) thickness. Press a whole walnut on top and bake for 15 to 16 minutes. Leave on the cookie sheets to cool completely.

BABY FUDGE BOMBS

When I was compiling all of my recipes for this cookbook, I texted my little sister Catherine after midnight (that's how texts to my sisters go) to find out what her favorite cookie was, and she wrote back, "My favorite cookie is a brownie." I promptly sent her a screenshot of this recipe that I've been making for years. These are just like brownies with the convenience of the cookie form. They're chewy and fudgy with a crackly shiny top, just like the best brownies should be. I like to keep them on the small side—like a two- or a three-bite treat. The recipe makes plenty, and they freeze beautifully. Catherine's little boy Walter keeps asking her to make "brownie cookies" now. They're a hit!

Makes 60 cookies

1 cup (200 g) granulated sugar

3 large eggs

8 oz (226 g) semisweet or dark chocolate chips

3 tbsp (42 g) unsalted butter

1½ tsp (8 ml) vanilla extract

½ tsp salt

½ tsp baking powder

1 cup (120 g) all-purpose flour, divided

In a large bowl, using a whisk, beat the sugar and eggs for 2 minutes, until they are thoroughly combined and the sugar has begun to dissolve. In a medium microwaveable bowl, heat the chocolate chips and butter on high for 1 minute. Stir. Continue to microwave in 30-second intervals until the chocolate and butter are completely smooth and melted. Pour the egg and sugar mixture into the hot chocolate mixture, whisking while you pour. Add the vanilla. Sprinkle the salt and baking powder over the dough. Stir for 1 minute. Add the flour and stir gently, just to combine. The dough will seem like a thick, sticky batter. Cover the bowl with plastic wrap and refrigerate for at least 2 hours, or up to 1 week.

Preheat the oven to 325°F (165°C). Line two baking sheets with parchment paper and lightly coat with cooking spray.

Shape the dough into ¾-inch (2-cm) balls and place on the prepared cookie sheets about 1½ inches (3.75 cm) apart. Bake for 7 to 10 minutes, or until the tops of the cookies are shiny and cracked—watching the cookies closely during the last few minutes of baking time. As soon as the cookies are cracked across the tops, they're done, so quickly take them out of the oven. Let the cookies cool for 5 minutes. Gently slide a spatula underneath to loosen the cookies and then leave them to cool completely on the baking sheets.

SOFT MOLASSES COOKIES

I adore a big, crinkly, molasses and spice cookie all year round, but especially in the early fall before the holidays come into full swing. I like these cookies heavy on the spice, so scale back if you want something more subtle. These cookies are best when cooled, so try to be patient when they come out of the oven. I don't want to be bossy, but do make these for a treat after a lunch of bacon, lettuce and tomato sandwiches on sourdough bread. You'll be so glad you did.

Makes 16 cookies

2 cups (400 g) granulated sugar, divided

¾ cup (170 g) unsalted butter, softened, (180 ml) canola oil or (140 g) vegetable shortening, softened

¼ cup (84 g) molasses

1 egg

1½ tsp (4 g) cinnamon

1 tsp ginger

¼ tsp cloves

½ tsp cardamom

¼ tsp nutmeg

¼ tsp salt

2½ tsp (12 g) baking soda

2 cups (250 g) all-purpose flour

Preheat the oven to 350°F (175°C). Line two or three baking sheets with parchment paper.

In a large bowl, combine 1 cup (200 g) of the sugar, the butter and the molasses. Add the egg and stir well. Sprinkle the cinnamon, ginger, cloves, cardamom, nutmeg, salt and baking soda over the dough and mix until well combined. Gently mix in the flour.

Shape the dough into 1-inch (2.5-cm) balls. Roll the balls in the remaining sugar and place on the prepared baking sheets. Bake for 8 to 11 minutes, or until the cookies are puffed and cracked. Let the cookies cool completely on the baking sheets.

DANISH BUTTER COOKIES

My dear friend Laura from New York sent me a P.S. on a text message. It said, "Do you have your own recipe for Danish butter cookies . . . you know, those little cookies that have been around since the '70s, come in the blue round tin and taste like heaven? If so WILL IT BE GOING IN YOUR COOKBOOK?" I will do anything for Laura, so I set to work. Danish cookies are in general less sweet and more buttery than their American counterparts, and as such the cookies are very simple, highly buttery and only lightly sweet. I always select the cookie that sparkles with coarse sugar, so that's the one that you'll get if you follow my recipe. For the prettiest shapes, don't make the cookie dough ahead of time; the dough needs to be piped as soon as it is stirred together, or it will become too thick to pipe. If that happens, the cookies would still be delicious rolled into little balls and flattened into rounds.

Makes 36 cookies

1 cup (227 g) unsalted butter, softened

½ cup (100 g) granulated sugar

½ tsp salt

1 tbsp (15 ml) vanilla extract

3 egg yolks

2 cups (250 g) all-purpose flour

¼ cup (50 g) coarse white sanding sugar

Preheat the oven to 350°F (175°C). Line two baking sheets with parchment paper.

In a large bowl, cream the butter and sugar together until very light and fluffy. Add the salt, vanilla and egg yolks, and mix well. Gently stir in the flour. Place the dough into a piping bag fitted with a ½-inch (1.25-cm) star. Alternately, you can just place the dough into a zip-top bag without a piping tip and snip a hole in the corner. Pipe the dough into little circle shapes about 3 inches (7.5 cm) in diameter. The size doesn't matter too much, but be sure that there is a hole in the center so that the cookies bake evenly. Sprinkle the cookies generously with the coarse sugar.

Bake for about 12 to 14 minutes, or until just turning golden brown on the bottoms. Let the cookies cool on the baking sheets for 5 minutes before transferring to a rack to cool completely.

CLASSIC VANILLA MERINGUES (GF)

I didn't even think I liked meringues until a neighbor brought them to a Christmas party at my parents' house a few years ago. After I tasted one, I ate as many as was socially acceptable, and then made a small plateful and hid them in my mom's pantry. My dad still claims he didn't even get one that night, since I had taken them all. Then I hounded the neighbor for her recipe, and the rest is history. I love that meringues are such a reasonable treat if you're watching your calories. One little meringue will set you back less than 25 calories. Don't you think you should have at least four now? A couple of meringue tips: Use an impeccably clean bowl and beaters to make sure there is no fat to keep the egg whites from puffing up large, and don't stop beating until you've got stiff peaks—but do stop there! I made all sorts of mistakes when I first started making meringues, but even the mistakes were delicious.

Makes about 20 meringues

2 large egg whites, room temperature

¼ tsp cream of tartar

Pinch of salt

½ cup (100 g) granulated sugar

1 tsp vanilla extract

Preheat the oven to 225°F (110°C). Line a large cookie sheet with parchment paper.

In a large bowl, using an electric mixer, beat the egg whites until foamy. Stir in the cream of tartar and pinch of salt. Continue to beat the egg whites, adding 1 tablespoon (15 g) of the sugar at a time, until the sugar is dissolved and the egg whites come to stiff peaks. This will take several minutes. Be patient and wait until they are stiff enough that if you pull up the beater the egg whites that slip off the beater can stand up straight on their own, without drooping over to the side. Add the vanilla and beat just long enough for it to get mixed in.

Transfer the meringue mixture to a piping bag fitted with a large star tip and pipe out the meringues onto a baking sheet, or simply spoon the meringues onto the baking sheet. You should have about 20 meringues. They can all fit onto one cookie sheet since they shouldn't spread much.

Bake for 1 hour. Turn off the oven and let the meringues sit in the oven, without opening the oven door, for an additional hour. Remove the meringues from the oven and allow to cool completely—which allows them to crisp—before eating.

PEANUT BUTTER AND STRAWBERRY THUMBPRINTS Ⓥ

I don't think a single soul will ever suspect that these cookies are vegan. The peanut butter cookie itself is tender, flavorful and just the right amount of crumbly. This is the only way that I make peanut butter thumbprints now, even if no one is eating vegan. These cookies are at their absolute best if you have homemade strawberry jam. It's really easy to freeze jam, so when the strawberries go on sale in the summertime, make a big batch and set some aside for these amazing cookies.

Makes about 30 cookies

½ cup (114 g) best quality vegan butter, softened

¾ cup (194 g) creamy peanut butter, not natural style

1¼ cups (250 g) granulated sugar, divided

¼ cup (55 g) brown sugar, packed

3 tbsp (45 ml) non-dairy milk

1 tsp vanilla extract

¼ tsp salt

½ tsp baking powder

½ tsp baking soda

2 cups (250 g) all-purpose flour

½ cup (160 g) strawberry jam

Preheat the oven to 350°F (175°C). Line two baking sheets with parchment paper.

In a large bowl, with an electric mixer, beat the butter and peanut butter until light and fluffy, about 2 minutes. Add ¾ cup (150 g) of the granulated sugar and the brown sugar and beat until well combined, about 2 minutes. Add the milk and vanilla. Sprinkle the salt, baking powder and baking soda over the dough and beat until a sticky dough forms. Switch to a wooden spoon and add the flour, mixing gently. Roll the dough into small balls, using about a tablespoon (14 g) of dough for each. Roll the balls gently in the remaining granulated sugar and place on the prepared baking sheets.

Bake the cookies for 10 minutes. Using the back of a spoon, press an indentation into the center of each cookie. Return to the oven and bake for 5 minutes. Immediately press the spoon into the cookies again to help keep the shape of the indentations.

Heat the jam in the microwave until it is warm and spreadable. Place ½ teaspoon of the jam into the indentation of each cookie. Let the cookies cool completely on the baking sheets. Store in an airtight container for up to a week.

BANANA CHOCOLATE CHIP COOKIES

These soft and cake-like cookies have a double hit of banana flavor from smashed,
ripe banana and sweetened banana chips. I tested this recipe with semisweet, milk chocolate,
white chocolate, peanut butter, butterscotch and caramel chips. I honestly could not decide
which chip was best—but I did like a little chip in every bite—so I wrote the recipe with
miniature semisweet chips. Feel free to use any kind of baking chip you like,
or even a combination of a few kinds.

Makes 36 cookies

½ cup (114 g) unsalted butter, softened

⅔ cup (145 g) brown sugar, packed

1 large egg

½ cup (113 g) mashed ripe banana (about 1 large)

1 tsp vanilla extract

½ tsp salt

1¼ tsp (6 g) baking powder

¼ tsp baking soda

1⅓ cups (166 g) all-purpose flour

1 cup (168 g) miniature semisweet chocolate chips

¾ cup (68 g) sweetened banana chips, coarsely chopped

½ cup (59 g) walnuts, toasted

Preheat the oven to 350°F (175°C). Line two baking sheets with parchment paper.

In a large bowl, cream the butter and sugar until light and fluffy. Add the egg, banana and vanilla. Sprinkle the salt, baking powder and baking soda over the dough. Mix well. Gently stir in the flour. Fold in the chocolate chips, banana chips and walnuts. Drop the dough, a tablespoonful (14 g) at a time, on the prepared baking sheets, about 2 inches (5 cm) apart. Bake for about 15 minutes, or until well set.

FUDGY CHOCOLATE BROWNIES
WITH TOASTED PECANS (v)

I wanted to bring some brownies to my vegan neighbor before she left on vacation, so I tried out a popular recipe—and it was just awful! This was a long time ago, when vegan baking was a new concept. The brownies had no flavor, no fudginess and no fun. I tried out a couple more recipes with the same luck, which is to say no luck at all. I decided to take matters into my own hands, and I set out to create a vegan brownie that would be so good that everyone, non-vegans too, would be happy to eat it. This is my brownie. I think you're going to love it. My two favorite vegan taste testers, Schneebs and Jordan, ate them right up and promptly texted me for the recipe, which is always a good sign.

Makes 12 brownies

2 tbsp (14 g) ground flaxseed

6 tbsp (90 ml) water, very hot

1 tsp baking soda

1 tsp white vinegar

½ cup (114 g) best quality vegan butter, softened, plus more for greasing the baking dish

¾ cup (165 g) brown sugar, packed

½ cup (100 g) granulated sugar

1 tbsp (15 ml) vanilla extract

¾ cup (66 g) cocoa powder

¼ tsp salt

1 tsp baking powder

1 cup (125 g) all-purpose flour

6 oz (170 g) vegan chocolate chips

1 cup (109 g) chopped toasted pecans

Preheat the oven to 350°F (175°C).

In a small bowl, whisk the flaxseed and water until smooth. Set aside for 10 minutes. In a separate small bowl, combine the baking soda and vinegar. Make sure the bowl is not too small since it will bubble up. In a large bowl, using an electric mixer or a wooden spoon, beat the butter, brown sugar and granulated sugar until light and fluffy, about 2 minutes. Add the flaxseed mixture, baking soda–vinegar mixture and vanilla and beat until well combined. Sprinkle the cocoa powder, salt and baking powder over the batter. Beat until there are no lumps and the mixture is smooth. Gently stir in the flour. Fold in the chocolate chips and pecans.

Lightly grease an 8 x 8-inch (20 x 20-cm) or 9 x 9-inch (23 x 23–cm) baking dish with butter. Pour the batter into the prepared baking dish and smooth the top with a rubber spatula.

Bake for 26 to 30 minutes, or until the edges are dark and the top is set. Remove from the oven to cool. The brownies will sink a little, but this will help them to be fudgy, not cakey.

Let the brownies cool for at least 20 minutes before cutting. I like these brownies best on the day they are made, but they're also delicious for a week, as long as they are kept in an airtight container.

A-LITTLE-BETTER-FOR-YOU
ICED MOLASSES COOKIES

You know, even when I'm trying to eat clean and healthy, I still demand treats. The last thing I eat before I go to bed has to be a sweet reward for making it through the day with my sanity intact. Maybe there's a causal relationship between sweet treats and sanity. I think the reason I haven't gone completely off my rocker is because sugar is my tranquilizer. Some say that sugar makes you hyper; I say it makes you calm. If you don't believe me, just try and withhold my sugar tonight, and you'll see a crazed, bulging-eyed woman in agitated crisis. I think, anyway. I've never gone without sugar, so this is all purely hypothetical. But why take any chances when so much peace and happiness hangs in the balance? Feed me, Seymour.

Makes 20 cookies

COOKIES

4 tbsp (56 g) unsalted butter, softened

½ cup (100 g) granulated sugar

½ cup (169 g) molasses

1 egg

1 tsp vanilla extract

⅛ tsp salt

½ tsp baking powder

¼ tsp baking soda

1 cup (90 g) old-fashioned oats

1 cup (120 g) whole wheat flour, plus more if needed

GLAZE

¼ cup (30 g) powdered sugar

1 to 2 tsp (5 to 10 ml) milk or orange juice

Preheat the oven to 350°F (175°C). Line a baking sheet with parchment paper.

To make the cookies, in a large bowl, cream the butter and sugar. Add the molasses and egg. Stir in the vanilla. Sprinkle in the salt, baking powder and baking soda, mixing well. Add the oats and flour and stir gently. The dough should be soft and slightly sticky, like the consistency of playdough. If the dough is too wet, add in more flour, 1 tablespoon (8 g) at a time. Roll the cookies into 1-inch (2.5-cm) balls and place them on the prepared baking sheet. Bake the cookies for 10 to 12 minutes, or until just set. Let cool for 5 minutes.

Prepare the glaze by combining the sugar and milk in a small bowl and mix until smooth. Drizzle the glaze on the warm cookies and serve. Because the cookies are lower in fat, I like them best when they are warm out of the oven, but they'll keep nicely in an airtight container for 3 to 4 days.

CLASSIC NO-BAKE CHOCOLATE PEANUT BUTTER COOKIES

My brother Roy got on a kick of making these cookies each week on Sunday after church. We were just kids, but this little brother of mine would whip up a batch of no-bake cookies for all of us to eat.

These cookies are easy to make, but you have to get a couple of things exactly right. The most important thing is the boiling time. When the mixture begins to bubble up almost to the center, it's boiling. Set your timer and wait exactly 1 minute. If your cookies are too wet, the mixture didn't boil long enough. If they are too dry, the mixture has boiled too long. Be absolutely precise with the minute of boiling time. The other trick is to measure your peanut butter in a measuring cup. I know, I know—why do I have to tell you this? It's because people (me) will try and take a shortcut and eyeball the amount of peanut butter instead of measuring. The success of the whole batch of cookies hangs in the balance. Don't make this mistake. Get out your measuring cup and measure the darn peanut butter, Erin.

Makes 24 cookies

½ cup (114 g) unsalted butter

2 cups (200 g) granulated sugar

Pinch of salt

¼ cup (22 g) cocoa powder

½ cup (120 ml) milk

½ cup (129 g) creamy peanut butter, not natural style

1 tsp vanilla extract

3 cups (270 g) quick-cooking oats

Lay out two sheets of waxed paper on a work surface.

In a medium saucepan, bring the butter, sugar, salt, cocoa powder and milk to a full rolling boil over medium heat, stirring often. Boil the mixture for 1 minute. Add the peanut butter, vanilla and oats.

Working quickly, drop the mixture by rounded teaspoonfuls (14 g) onto the waxed paper. Let the cookies cool completely to harden. Since these cookies are going to be irregularly sized, if you need them to be more standard in shape, try dropping the mixture not onto waxed paper, but into paper-lined muffin tins. They are easier to portion and share this way.

PUMPKIN SNICKERDOODLES

Snickerdoodles are fun, but pumpkin snickerdoodles are pure autumnal fun. These fall favorites are vegan because they don't contain any dairy or animal products, but if you're not vegan and you don't have vegan butter on hand, you can make these with regular butter and they'll come out great too! The pumpkin puree here not only flavors the cookies and gives them a nice warm color, but also serves as a natural stand-in for eggs. The cookies are rolled not in the traditional cinnamon and sugar, but in pumpkin pie spice and sugar for an extra hit of autumn!

Makes about 48 cookies

COOKIES

1 cup (227 g) best quality vegan butter or (190 g) vegetable shortening, softened

1⅔ cups (332 g) granulated sugar

¾ cup (180 ml) pumpkin puree

2 tsp (10 ml) vanilla extract

1 tsp pumpkin pie spice

½ tsp salt

1½ tsp (7 g) baking soda

1 tsp cream of tartar

3 cups (375 g) all-purpose flour, plus more if needed

TOPPING

4 tbsp (50 g) granulated sugar

2 tsp (5 g) pumpkin pie spice

1 tbsp (8 g) cinnamon

Preheat the oven to 400°F (205°C). Line two baking sheets with parchment paper.

To make the cookies, in a large bowl, beat the butter and sugar until light and fluffy. Add the pumpkin puree and vanilla. Sprinkle the pumpkin pie spice, salt, baking soda and cream of tartar over the dough. Beat for 1 minute, or until well incorporated. Gently stir in the flour. The dough should be slightly sticky. If the dough is too sticky to roll into a ball, add more flour, a tablespoon (8 g) at a time, until the dough is workable.

To prepare the topping, in a small bowl, combine the sugar, pumpkin pie spice and cinnamon. Roll the dough into ping-pong-sized balls. Roll each dough ball generously in the sugar mixture. I like to roll the ball in the sugar mixture, then re-roll it back into a good ball shape since they flatten out a little when you roll them in the sugar.

Place the balls on the prepared baking sheets and bake for 7 to 9 minutes, or until just set. Do not overbake. Let the cookies cool on the baking sheets for 5 minutes. Transfer to a rack to cool completely.

CARAMEL COOKIES WITH CORNFLAKES, MARSHMALLOWS AND PEANUT BUTTER M&M'S

Sometimes on my birthday I get Peanut Butter M&M's from every person in my family. I must be really easy to buy a gift for. It's no secret how much I love them, and by extension, anyone who buys them for me. I crammed this cookie full of all the sweet, salty and crunchy flavors and textures that I crave—like my beloved Peanut Butter M&M's. They're my favorite candy, but they need to be added to a big, sturdy cookie that can stand up to their bumpy shape. It's also important to use frozen marshmallows in this cookie so that they keep their shape and don't melt into the cookie, but the truth is that stale marshmallows work really well too. The caramel flavor comes through from both the dark brown sugar and generous hit of molasses.

Makes 10–12 cookies

½ cup (114 g) unsalted butter, softened

¾ cup (165 g) dark brown sugar, packed

¼ cup (50 g) granulated sugar

2 tsp (10 ml) vanilla extract

1 tbsp (20 g) molasses

1 egg

¾ tsp salt

½ tsp baking soda

½ tsp baking powder

1⅓ cups (166 g) all-purpose flour

¾ cup (21 g) cornflakes, or Frosted Flakes cereal, crushed

¾ cup (38 g) stale or frozen miniature marshmallows

¾ cup (126 g) candy-coated peanut butter chocolates, divided (I recommend Peanut Butter M&M's)

Preheat the oven to 350°F (175°C). Line two baking sheets with parchment paper.

In a large bowl, cream the butter, dark brown sugar and granulated sugar until light and fluffy. Add the vanilla, molasses and egg, mixing until well combined. Stir in the salt, baking soda and baking powder, stirring until well combined. Add the flour, mixing gently until just blended. Stir in the cornflakes, marshmallows and ½ cup (84 g) of the candy-coated peanut butter chocolates.

Scoop the cookie dough into generous ¼-cup (56-g) balls. You should have between 10 and 12 cookies. Place on the cookie sheets with 2 inches (5 cm) of space between. Bake for about 10 minutes, or until the tops are just beginning to caramelize. Remove from the oven and immediately poke the remaining candy-coated peanut butter chocolates into the still-warm cookies. Let the cookies cool on the baking sheets for 10 minutes, then transfer to a rack. These cookies are equally good warm and at room temperature, but if you want to keep the cornflakes crunchy, wait until the cookies cool to room temperature before eating.

ITALIAN WEDDING COOKIES

Talk about a cookie with a million different aliases! I've seen these, and other slight variations, called snowballs, Russian tea cakes, Mexican wedding cakes, Italian wedding cookies, butterballs, polvorones, biscochitos and even pecan Susans. Am I missing any names? Maybe I should just make up one of my own and add it to the list. Who would even notice? Or maybe I'm just going to call them Italian wedding cookies as a nod to my Italian heritage. We Italians like to claim all the best food as ours! The secret to the best cookies, whatever you call them, is to roll them twice in powdered sugar—once when they are warm, and then again when they are cooled.

Makes 48 cookies

1 cup (227 g) unsalted butter, softened

¼ cup (50 g) granulated sugar

1½ tsp (8 ml) vanilla extract

½ tsp salt

2 cups (250 g) all-purpose flour

2 cups (218 g) finely chopped toasted pecans

2 cups (240 g) powdered sugar

Preheat the oven to 325°F (165°C). Line two baking sheets with parchment paper.

In a large bowl, beat the butter and sugar until light and creamy. Stir in the vanilla. Add the salt and flour, stirring gently. Fold in the pecans. Shape the dough into 1-inch (2.5-cm) balls and place on the prepared cookie sheets at least 1 inch (2.5 cm) apart. Bake for about 15 to 18 minutes, or until just beginning to brown. Let the cookies cool for 5 minutes, then toss them in the powdered sugar. Remove to a rack to cool completely, then toss again in the powdered sugar.

SEA SALT BROWN BUTTER DELUXE CRISPY RICE TREATS

These are the big, fat, chunky rice cereal treats that you see for sale at bakeries and coffee shops, only these are so much better because they are fresh, buttery and full of both swirls of melted marshmallow and pockets of marshmallow pieces. Take your time with the brown butter to make sure you get the deepest flavor, but don't take a phone call or multitask because browned butter goes from perfect to burnt in a matter of seconds. I also like a little hit of maple extract here to complement the browned butter, but it's optional! Don't skip the bit of sea salt on top for an elegant finish. Also, this might seem a little fussy, but I do think the best treats come from an unopened box of cereal and very fresh marshmallows that aren't sticking together in the package. I know, I know, it's fussy, but I think you'll be pleased if you make them just right.

Makes 24 crispy rice treats

½ cup (114 g) unsalted butter, plus more for greasing the pan

2 (10-oz [283-g]) bags miniature marshmallows, divided

1 tsp vanilla extract

½ tsp maple extract, optional

½ tsp salt

9 cups (192 g) crispy rice cereal

Sea salt, for finishing

You have two choices for pan size. You can use a jelly roll pan for a thinner treat, or you can use a 9 x 13–inch (23 x 33–cm) pan, preferably one that has straight sides and not rounded corners. Whichever one you decide to use, grease it lightly with butter. Place 1 bag of marshmallows in the freezer while you're preparing the treats. It'll be less than 10 minutes.

In a large pot over low heat, melt the butter. Increase the heat to medium and using a wooden spoon, stir the butter as it cooks, scraping up any brown bits. The butter will melt, then foam, then start to create little brown specks at the bottom. You want the butter to turn a medium golden brown with brown specks. Watch it carefully because you don't want any burned black specks. Turn off the heat and add the room temperature bag of marshmallows to the pot. Stir until the marshmallows are smooth. Add the vanilla extract and maple extract, if using. Stir in the salt. Quickly add the rice cereal and stir until well blended. Remove the marshmallows from the freezer and quickly stir them into the mixture. You want them to melt just a little, but remain mostly intact.

Using slightly damp hands, press the treats into the prepared baking dish. Sprinkle the top with a little sea salt. Let the treats rest for at least 90 minutes at room temperature so they have a chance to firm up. Spray your knife with cooking spray before cutting the treats into squares.

MINI CHOCOLATE CHIP CUTIES

I started making these bite-size cookies for a family New Year's Eve party over a decade ago. My adorable little nieces Claire and Eloise just absolutely loved them. Whenever they came into town for our party they asked me to make them again, and pretty soon it just became a tradition. That said, I will make them for Claire and Eloise, who are now grown up but still adorable teenagers, whenever they come around, even if it isn't New Year's Eve. It takes a bit of work to roll all the dough into tiny balls, but hopefully you can enlist a tiny—or a teenaged—helper or two.

Makes about 80 tiny cookies

½ cup (114 g) unsalted butter, softened

⅔ cup (132 g) granulated sugar

⅓ cup (73 g) brown sugar, packed

1 egg

2 tsp (10 ml) vanilla extract

½ tsp salt

½ tsp baking powder

¾ tsp baking soda

1½ cups (188 g) all-purpose flour

1 cup (168 g) miniature chocolate chips

Preheat the oven to 350°F (175°C). Line two baking sheets with parchment paper.

In a large bowl, using a wooden spoon, cream the butter, granulated sugar and brown sugar until light and creamy, about 3 minutes. Add in the egg and vanilla. Once the egg and vanilla are incorporated, sprinkle the salt, baking powder and baking soda over the cookie dough and mix well. Gently add the flour and stir until just combined. Stir in the chocolate chips. Shape the dough into small balls, roughly the size of grapes, and place on the cookie sheets with about an inch (2.5 cm) of space between them.

Bake the cookies for about 6 to 9 minutes, or until just golden brown on the edges. Don't overbake. They should be soft and tender. Let the cookies cool completely on the cookie sheets and then pile them onto a giant platter for serving.

LUCKY CHARMS COOKIES

When my kids were little I only let them have sugar cereals on special occasions. For St. Patrick's Day I would always buy a big box of Lucky Charms for breakfast. After a while we started to associate Lucky Charms with St. Paddy's Day. They're hardly Irish, but I think we Americans like them for our St. Patrick's Day celebrations. After all, there is a leprechaun on the box, and he does have an Irish brogue on the commercial. Authentic or not, the cereal makes adorable, colorful cookies that are magically delicious. If you can find the special edition green marshmallows box for St. Patrick's Day, buy it up!

Makes about 24 cookies

½ cup (114 g) unsalted butter, softened

½ cup (110 g) brown sugar, packed

1 egg

1 tsp vanilla extract

½ tsp salt

½ tsp baking powder

½ tsp baking soda

4 cups (144 g) toasted oat cereal with marshmallows, such as Lucky Charms, to produce 1 cup (50 g) marshmallows and 1½ cups (82 g) of cereal flour (see Tip)

½ cup (63 g) all-purpose flour

½ cup (84 g) white chocolate chips, plus more for poking into the tops of the cookies

Preheat the oven to 350°F (175°C). Line two baking sheets with parchment paper.

In a large bowl, cream together the butter and sugar until light and fluffy. Add the egg and vanilla. Sprinkle the salt, baking powder and baking soda over the top. Mix well. Add the cereal flour and all-purpose flour, stirring gently. Fold in the chocolate chips and half of the marshmallows.

Roll the dough into 24 small ping-pong-sized balls. Divide on the baking sheets and bake for about 7 to 8 minutes, or until just set but not yet firm. Remove from the oven. Immediately poke the remaining marshmallows and chocolate chips into the tops of the hot cookies. Let the cookies cool completely before serving.

Tip: *To make the cereal flour, first separate the marshmallows and the cereal. Pulse the dry cereal in a blender or food processor until it is ground into a fine powder. Set any remaining flour aside for making cookies another time.*

PEEKABOO RASPBERRY JAM SANDWICH COOKIES

Peekaboo isn't a serious enough name for this stunner of a cookie. They're just the prettiest buttery sandwich cookies with a sprinkle of powdered sugar on the top and a window to peek in and see the shiny jam. The best way to make these cookies shine is to use a few different flavors of jam. My favorites are raspberry, apricot, peach and blackberry, but I've even ventured away from jams to use lemon curd, chocolate hazelnut spread and caramel with a sprinkle of sea salt.

Makes about 36 cookies

COOKIES

1 cup (227 g) unsalted butter, softened

1 cup (200 g) granulated sugar

½ cup (60 g) powdered sugar

2 eggs

1½ tsp (8 ml) vanilla extract

½ tsp lemon extract, optional

½ tsp salt

1 tsp baking powder

½ tsp baking soda

3 cups (375 g) all-purpose flour, plus more for the work surface

FILLING & TOPPING

½ cup (60 g) powdered sugar

¾ cup (240 g) jam, any flavor, but preferably at least 2 flavors in contrasting colors, such as apricot and raspberry

To make the cookies, in a large bowl, using an electric mixer, beat the butter, granulated sugar and powdered sugar until light and fluffy, about 2 minutes. Add the eggs, vanilla and lemon extract, if using, and beat on high until well combined, about 1 minute. Sprinkle the salt, baking powder and baking soda over the top and beat until well combined. Switch to a wooden spoon. Gently stir in the flour until just combined. Gather the dough into a ball and wrap tightly in plastic wrap. Chill for 2 hours, or up to 1 week.

When you're ready to bake, preheat the oven to 350°F (175°C). Line two baking sheets with parchment paper.

Roll the dough out onto a lightly floured surface to ¼-inch (6-mm) thickness. Using a 3-inch (7.5-cm) round cutter, cut the dough into cookies, re-rolling the scraps as necessary. For half of the cookies, cut out a small shape at the center of the cookie so that you can see the jam later. I like to use the round edge of a cake piping tip for cutting out a small center circle, but a very small cookie cutter would also work. These will be the top cookies, and the cookies with the center intact will be the bottoms. Place the cut cookies on the prepared baking sheets with an inch (2.5 cm) of space between them. I like to put all the top cookies on one baking sheet, and all the bottom cookies on the other.

Bake for 12 to 14 minutes, or until the edges are just golden brown. Allow the cookies to rest on the baking sheets until cooled completely.

To make the filling and topping, sift the powdered sugar over the tops of only the cookies that have a cutout in the center. Spread the jams on the bottoms of the cookies with no cutout. Place a cutout cookie on top of a jam-covered cookie to create a sandwich with a peekaboo. Repeat the process with the remaining cookies. Store the cookies for up to 5 days in an airtight container.

TAKE FIVE BROWNIES

Five powerhouse ingredients—milk chocolate, peanuts, caramel, peanut butter and pretzels—top these brownies. I am not a fan of layered, over-the-top stunt-type desserts if they don't keep a careful balance. These brownies are rich and packed full of delicious layers, but there's a precise balance of chocolaty decadence, silky peanut butter caramel and textural crunch and steadying salt from the pretzels and peanuts. I like to cut these small to emphasize the fact that they are a special, indulgent treat—but cut them big and go bold, if that's your style.

Makes 18 brownies

BROWNIES

½ cup (114 g) unsalted butter, plus more for greasing the pan

1 cup (200 g) granulated sugar

2 large eggs

½ tsp vanilla extract

¼ tsp salt

½ tsp baking powder

⅓ cup (27 g) cocoa powder

½ cup (63 g) all-purpose flour

TOPPING

½ cup (100 g) granulated sugar

½ cup (120 ml) water

1 cup (240 ml) heavy cream

2 tbsp (30 ml) corn syrup or honey

1 cup (258 g) creamy peanut butter

1 tsp vanilla extract

⅛ tsp salt

2 cups (80 g) waffle-style pretzels, divided

½ cup (73 g) chopped peanuts

4 oz (113 g) milk chocolate candy melts or melting wafers, melted

Preheat the oven to 350°F (175°C). Line an 8 x 8-inch (20 x 20-cm) pan with parchment paper and lightly grease the parchment.

To make the brownies, place the butter in a large microwaveable bowl and microwave on high until the butter is just melted. Add the sugar and mix well. Add the eggs and vanilla. Sprinkle the salt, baking powder and cocoa powder over the top and mix for 1 minute, or until no lumps remain. Add the flour and gently stir. Pour the mixture into the prepared baking dish and bake for 25 to 30 minutes, or until the top is raised and a toothpick inserted into the center comes out with only a few fudgy crumbs. Let the brownies cool completely.

Using the back of a wooden spoon, poke about 16 holes into the brownies, about ½ inch (1.25 cm) deep. This will help the caramel sink into the brownies a bit. When the brownies are cooled, make the peanut butter caramel.

To make the topping, in a medium saucepan over medium heat, heat the sugar and the water, without stirring, until the mixture turns light brown. You can pick up the pan and carefully swirl it from time to time. The process usually takes about 4 to 7 minutes. When the sugar mixture is a light brown caramel color, slowly add the cream and cook for 1 minute, stirring constantly so the cream can be thoroughly blended into the caramel. Remove from the heat and stir in the corn syrup, peanut butter, vanilla and salt.

Pour half of the caramel over the brownies. Add a single layer of pretzels over the caramel, pressing in to adhere. Pour the remaining caramel over the pretzels. Chop any remaining pretzels that you have into small bits until you have about ⅓ cup (20 g) of pretzel crumbs. Sprinkle the top of the caramel with the pretzel crumbs and peanuts. Refrigerate until the caramel is set, about 1 hour. Drizzle with the melted chocolate and cut into pieces.

OATMEAL, BUTTERSCOTCH AND TOFFEE COOKIES WITH SEA SALT

I didn't know I was such a fan of oatmeal cookies until I started gathering my favorite recipes together to create this cookbook. So many of the cookies that I love have a wholesome addition of oats. It kind of makes me feel like a horse—just give me a bucket of oats, or oatmeal cookies, every night and I'll be happy in my stall.

I know that lots of people love their oatmeal cookies with raisins, but I think oatmeal cookies are even better with butterscotch and pecans. Actually, I like the raisin cookies too. I like anything with oats—see above horse comment. There's a lot of buttery sweetness in these cookies, so chop the butterscotch fairly small so that the flavors stay balanced and don't shy away from the sea salt on top.

Makes 12 cookies

½ cup (114 g) unsalted butter, softened

¾ cup (165 g) dark brown sugar, packed

½ cup (100 g) granulated sugar

¾ tsp vanilla extract

1 egg

½ tsp salt

½ tsp baking powder

½ tsp baking soda

¾ cup (94 g) all-purpose flour

1½ cups (135 g) quick-cooking oats

½ cup (55 g) chopped toasted pecans, plus more for the tops of the cookies

½ cup (84 g) butterscotch chips, coarsely chopped

¼ cup (42 g) toffee bits

Sea salt, for finishing

Preheat the oven to 350°F (175°C). Line two baking sheets with parchment paper.

In a large bowl, cream together the butter, brown sugar and granulated sugar until light and creamy. Add the vanilla and egg and mix well. Sprinkle the salt, baking powder and baking soda over the top of the dough and mix to combine. Very gently stir in the flour and the oats. The dough will be sticky and thick. Add the pecans, butterscotch chips and toffee bits. Shape the dough into golf ball–sized balls. Place on the prepared cookie sheets.

Bake for about 8 minutes, or until just beginning to brown on the edges. Sprinkle the hot cookies with sea salt and poke extra pecans into the tops. Let the cookies rest on the baking sheets until completely cooled.

PEPPERMINT SUGAR COOKIES

I never in a million years dreamed that a vanilla-mint frosted cookie with shards
of peppermint would top my list of holiday cookie favorites. It's all chocolate's fault. If chocolate
is around, then I'm of a single-track mind. I'm so glad I turned my back on chocolate—
temporarily—to try this gem of a treat! I like to frost some of my cookies pink and some of my
cookies green with both green and red chopped candy canes on top.

Makes 20 cookies

COOKIES

½ cup (114 g) unsalted butter,
softened

¼ cup (60 ml) vegetable oil

4 tbsp (60 ml) sour cream

1 cup (200 g) granulated sugar

1 egg

1 tsp vanilla extract

½ tsp salt

½ tsp baking powder

½ tsp baking soda

2½ cups (313 g) all-purpose flour

½ cup (84 g) mint baking chips,
or coarsely chopped candy canes

FROSTING

¼ cup (57 g) unsalted butter,
softened

4 oz (113 g) cream cheese, softened

1 tsp peppermint extract

½ tsp vanilla extract

1 tbsp (15 ml) milk

2 cups (240 g) powdered sugar

Pink and/or green food coloring,
optional

½ cup (116 g) crushed candy
canes or peppermints, for
sprinkling

Preheat the oven to 350°F (175°C). Line two baking sheets with
parchment paper.

To make the cookies, in a large bowl, cream together the butter,
oil, sour cream and sugar until light and fluffy. Add the egg
and vanilla. Sprinkle the salt, baking powder and baking soda
over the dough. Mix well. Gently stir in the flour. Fold in the
mint chips. Using about 2 tablespoons (28 g) of the dough for
each ball, shape the dough into 20 balls. Place the balls on the
prepared cookie sheets, about 2 inches (5 cm) apart. Smash the
balls evenly with the bottom of a drinking glass. The edges
should be jagged.

Bake the cookies for about 8 to 10 minutes, or until just set. Let
the cookies cool on the baking sheets for 5 minutes, and then
transfer to a rack to cool completely.

Prepare the frosting by combining the butter, cream cheese,
peppermint extract, vanilla, milk and powdered sugar. Beat well
until the frosting is thick and fluffy. Add the food coloring, if
using. I like to divide my frosting in half and tint half pink, and
the other half green. Frost the cookies and sprinkle with the
crushed candy canes.

PEANUT BUTTER COOKIES WITH CHOCOLATE FROSTING

It's funny, I don't like chocolate chips in my peanut butter cookies. It seems like chocolate chips disrupt the crumbly, pleasing sandy texture of a PB cookie. Still, I love the combo of chocolate and peanut butter. My daughter Sailor started adding chocolate frosting to peanut butter cookies, which keeps the integrity of the texture, but provides a luxurious schmear of chocolaty goodness.

Makes about 48 cookies

COOKIES

½ cup (114 g) unsalted butter, softened

¾ cup (194 g) creamy peanut butter, not natural style

1 cup (220 g) brown sugar, packed

1 egg

2 tsp (10 ml) vanilla extract

½ tsp salt

½ tsp baking soda

1½ cups (188 g) all-purpose flour

½ cup (100 g) granulated sugar, for rolling the cookies

FROSTING

2 tbsp (28 g) unsalted butter

2 tbsp (11 g) cocoa powder

2 tbsp (30 ml) milk

½ tsp vanilla extract

2 cups (240 g) powdered sugar, plus more if needed

Preheat the oven to 350°F (175°C). Line two or three baking sheets with parchment paper.

To prepare the cookies, in a large bowl, cream together the butter, peanut butter and brown sugar until light and fluffy. Add the egg and vanilla. Sprinkle the salt and baking soda over the dough. Mix well. Gently stir in the flour. Shape the dough into 1-inch (2.5-cm) balls and roll in the granulated sugar. Place about 2 inches (5 cm) apart on the cookie sheets. Using the bottom of a drinking glass, flatten the cookies slightly. Bake until just set and beginning to brown on the edges, about 7 to 9 minutes. Let the cookies cool on the cookie sheets for about 5 minutes before transferring to a rack to cool completely.

To prepare the frosting, combine the butter, cocoa powder and milk in a medium saucepan over medium heat, stirring constantly. Boil for 1 minute. Remove from the heat and stir in the vanilla and powdered sugar. Add more powdered sugar as needed to form a thick frosting. Frost each of the cooled cookies generously and let sit until the chocolate is set.

MARY KATE'S SOFT OATMEAL MILK CHOCOLATE CHIP COOKIES

I left for college when my baby sister Mary Kate was only seven years old. It was my saddest goodbye. She was such a charming little girl, and I was worried she would grow up and not be as charming while I was gone. It turns out I had nothing to worry about. I never walk into Mary Kate's house without finding a batch of cookie dough whirring in her mixer and at least two of her kids, usually the twins Jane and Michael, licking a spatula in the kitchen.
These are my favorite cookies that charming MK makes.

Makes about 36 cookies

1 cup (227 g) unsalted butter, softened

½ cup (100 g) granulated sugar

1 cup (220 g) dark brown sugar, packed

2 eggs

2 tsp (10 ml) vanilla extract

1 tsp salt

½ tsp baking soda

1½ cups (188 g) all-purpose flour

3 cups (270 g) quick-cooking oats (look for the kind that cooks in 1 minute)

2 cups (336 g) semisweet chocolate chips, divided

Preheat the oven to 325°F (165°C). Line two or three baking sheets with parchment paper.

In a large bowl or free-standing mixer, beat the butter, granulated sugar and brown sugar until light and creamy. Mix in the eggs and vanilla. Sprinkle the salt and baking soda over the dough and beat for 1 minute. Gently stir in the flour and oats. Fold in 1 cup (168 g) of the chocolate chips. Using generous tablespoons (15 g) of dough, roll into balls. Bake for exactly 10 minutes. Immediately poke the remaining chocolate chips into the tops of the cookies. Let the cookies cool on the baking sheets for about 6 minutes, then transfer to a rack to cool completely.

GLAZED CINNAMON ROLL COOKIES

Don't let the tiny little bit of yeast in this cookie scare you away. You don't have to do anything special. You can treat it like any other dry ingredient—just throw it in the dough when you add your salt. The little bit of yeast is going to give these cookies a tiny bit of lift and a little bit of the raised dough flavor that you associate with fluffy, homemade cinnamon rolls. They take a little bit of patience since the dough needs to chill for at least 4 hours. I usually just make them the day before. I love these cookies with a traditional vanilla glaze on top, but I also love them with an orange glaze (just add a teaspoon of orange zest and use orange juice instead of milk), or a maple glaze (trade the vanilla for maple extract). These might be my mom's favorite cookies in the whole book. She loves to tell her friends about them.

Makes about 36 cookies

COOKIES

½ cup (114 g) unsalted butter, softened

½ cup (100 g) granulated sugar

1 egg

½ tsp vanilla extract

¼ tsp salt

½ tsp active dry or rapid rise yeast

½ tsp baking powder

1⅓ cups (166 g) all-purpose flour, plus more for the work surface and as needed

¼ cup (55 g) brown sugar, packed

2 tsp (5 g) cinnamon

GLAZE

¾ cup (90 g) powdered sugar

1 tsp vanilla extract

2 tbsp (30 ml) milk

To make the cookies, in a large bowl, cream the butter and sugar until light and fluffy. Add the egg and vanilla. Sprinkle the salt, yeast and baking powder over the top. Mix well. Gently stir in the flour. The dough should be the texture of playdough. Add additional flour as necessary, a tablespoon (8 g) at a time, until the dough is only just slightly sticky.

On a lightly floured surface, roll out the dough into a 15 x 7–inch (38 x 18–cm) rectangle. Sprinkle the dough with the brown sugar and cinnamon. Roll up the dough, starting with the long edge, into a cylinder. The dough might tear a little, but just keep patiently working and rolling. Any little rips will not show up in the final product. Pinch the dough to seal it tightly at the seam. Wrap the dough in waxed paper and place in the fridge. The cylinder of dough usually stretches a little. I notice that it's usually about 18 inches (46 cm) long by the time I get it to the fridge. Chill the dough for at least 4 hours, or up to 1 week.

When ready to bake, preheat the oven to 350°F (175°C). Line two baking sheets with parchment paper.

Slice the dough into ½-inch (1.25-cm) rounds and place on the baking sheets. Bake until just set and golden brown on the bottom, around 8 to 10 minutes.

Prepare the glaze by combining the powdered sugar, vanilla and milk until smooth. Dip the top of the cooled cookies in the glaze.

SALTED CARAMEL APPLE COOKIES

Once I made a batch of these cookies with some caramel bits that I found in the back of the cupboard. I don't have any idea how old those bits were, but I do know that they could have potentially broken a tooth. They were rock hard! I didn't find out until I bit into the first cookie and my face crumpled into a grimace. That was it. I stopped making these with caramel bits and switched to toffee bits and caramel baking chips, which I think are even tastier with the fresh apple. Caramel baking chips are getting easier to find now, and if you're lucky you might even be able to find sea salt caramel chips—my favorite.

Makes 24 cookies

½ cup (114 g) unsalted butter, softened

½ cup (100 g) granulated sugar

¼ cup (55 g) dark brown sugar, packed

1 egg

1 tsp vanilla extract

1 tsp cinnamon

½ tsp allspice

¼ tsp nutmeg

½ tsp salt

½ tsp baking powder

½ tsp baking soda

1½ cups (188 g) all-purpose flour

1 medium apple, peeled, cored and cut into a ¼-inch (6-mm) dice (I like Granny Smith)

1¼ cups (210 g) caramel chips, divided

½ cup (84 g) toffee chips

Sea salt, for finishing

Preheat the oven to 350°F (175°C). Line two baking sheets with parchment paper and coat lightly with cooking spray.

In a large bowl, cream the butter, granulated sugar and brown sugar until light and fluffy. Add the egg and vanilla. Sprinkle the cinnamon, allspice, nutmeg, salt, baking powder and baking soda over the dough. Mix for 1 minute. Gently stir in the flour. Fold in the apple, ¾ cup (126 g) of the caramel chips and the toffee chips. Shape the dough into ping-pong-sized balls and place on the prepared cookie sheets with 2 inches (5 cm) of space between them.

Bake for 7 to 9 minutes, or until just set. Immediately remove from the oven, poke in the remaining caramel chips and sprinkle with the sea salt. Let the cookies cool for 5 minutes on the baking sheets before removing to a rack to cool completely.

CHOCOLATE PEANUT BUTTER CUPS, CHIPS AND PIECES COOKIES

When I was a kid, I wouldn't eat any Reese's Pieces because I didn't like the color scheme. I had a grudge against orange and brown because my great-grandmother would sew brown and orange dresses for me. She thought the colors looked good with my brown hair and brown eyes. Never mind that my blonde-haired, green-eyed sister Michelle got all the pink and blue dresses. But my grandma was the nicest soul alive, and I'm sure I was a devilish little ingrate. Sorry, Great Grandma. I'm nicer now, promise. I didn't start eating Reese's Pieces until I saw the movie *ET* in the theaters. Only then could I forgive the orange and brown color scheme enough to enjoy what is now one of my very favorite candies, and hence one of my favorite cookies. It's a good thing I got over my color grudge, because Reese's Pieces are out of this world.

Makes 24 cookies

½ cup (114 g) unsalted butter, softened

¼ cup plus 2 tbsp (83 g) brown sugar, packed

⅓ cup (66 g) granulated sugar

¾ tsp vanilla extract

1 egg

¼ tsp salt

¼ tsp baking powder

½ tsp baking soda

⅓ cup (27 g) cocoa powder

1 cup (125 g) all-purpose flour

½ cup (60 g) chopped peanut butter cups (I recommend Reese's Peanut Butter Cups)

¾ cup (126 g) peanut butter chips, divided

1 cup (188 g) candy-coated peanut butter chocolates, divided (I recommend Reese's Pieces)

Preheat the oven to 350°F (175°C). Line two baking sheets with parchment paper.

In a large bowl, combine the butter, brown sugar and granulated sugar, creaming until light and fluffy. Stir in the vanilla and egg. Sprinkle the salt, baking powder, baking soda and cocoa powder over the dough. Mix until no lumps remain and the mixture is smooth. Gently stir in the flour. The dough will be sticky. This is necessary to hold in all of the mix-ins. Fold in the peanut butter cups, half of the peanut butter chips and half of the candy-coated peanut butter chocolates. Drop the cookies by tablespoonfuls (14 g) onto the prepared baking sheets, spacing a couple of inches (5 cm) apart.

Bake for 7 to 9 minutes. Immediately poke in the remaining peanut butter chips and candy-coated peanut butter chocolates on top of the cookies. Let the cookies cool for 5 minutes on the baking sheets before transferring to a rack to cool completely.

PINK AND WHITE CIRCUS ANIMAL COOKIES

Are there any children that don't love pink and white candy-coated animal cookies with colorful sprinkles? I once asked my little nephew Gio if I could bring him some homemade cookies after his baby brother Teo was born. I thought Gio would be delighted, but instead he told me that the only cookies he liked were circus animal cookies. That was it! But you know, I think he was on to something because there is something special and fun about these little childhood favorites. The packaged cookies are good, I admit, but these are so much better because they are both fresh and buttery. You can also make them with whatever color candy coating and sprinkles that you want, so the possibilities are endless. These would be so fun with green candy coating and red and white sprinkles at Christmas, or orange candy coating and black and white sprinkles for Halloween. You get the idea!

Makes about 40 cookies

½ cup (114 g) unsalted butter, softened

1 cup (120 g) powdered sugar

1 egg

½ tsp vanilla extract

½ tsp almond extract

¼ tsp salt

½ tsp baking powder

¼ tsp baking soda

1½ cups (188 g) all-purpose flour, plus more for the work surface

1 cup (168 g) pink candy melts

1 cup (168 g) white candy melts

Small rainbow sprinkles

In a large bowl, using a wooden spoon, cream the butter and powdered sugar together until light and fluffy, about 3 minutes. Stir in the egg, vanilla and almond extract. Sprinkle the salt, baking powder and baking soda over the dough and stir well. Add the flour and stir gently until just combined. Gather the dough into a ball and wrap tightly with plastic wrap. Refrigerate for 2 hours, or up to 1 week.

When ready to bake, preheat the oven to 350°F (175°C). Line two baking sheets with parchment paper.

On a lightly floured work surface, roll out the dough to ¼-inch (6-mm) thickness. Using small animal cookie cutters, or any small cookie cutter of your choice, cut the cookies and arrange on the prepared baking sheets with 2 inches (5 cm) of space between them.

Bake for 10 to 12 minutes, or until just starting to become golden brown on the edges. Cool the cookies on the baking sheets.

When completely cooled, melt the pink and white candy melts separately in microwaveable bowls, in 30-second intervals, stirring until completely melted and smooth. Spread either the pink or the white candy melts on the top of each cookie and immediately top with the colorful sprinkles (use plenty!) before the candy melt sets atop the cookie. My preferred method is to dip the tops of the cookies into the candy melt. Let the cookies cool and set completely before serving. If you're in a rush, put them in the fridge for a bit. Store in an airtight container and share with any young—or young-at-heart—person that you love.

LIME-IN-THE-COCONUT COOKIES

Every year for Father's Day my daughter Sailor makes a key lime pie for her dad.
Shane looks forward to his special pie every year. But after Father's Day we are all
still craving lime, and we can't make the pie because that is THE Father's Day ONLY dessert.
Now we make key lime and coconut cookies instead, and let me tell you, they are exactly the
dessert you need for all your BBQs and swim parties. You might as well print up
the recipe now, because everyone is going to ask you for it.

Makes about 28 cookies

COOKIES

½ cup (114 g) unsalted butter, softened

¾ cup (150 g) granulated sugar

1 egg

½ tsp coconut extract

1 tbsp (10 g) lime zest

1 tbsp (15 ml) lime juice

¼ tsp salt

1 tsp baking powder

1¼ cups (156 g) all-purpose flour

GLAZE

1¼ cups (150 g) powdered sugar

2 tbsp (30 ml) fresh lime juice

½ tsp coconut extract

¼ cup (23 g) sweetened shredded coconut, for sprinkling on the tops of the cookies

1 tbsp (10 g) lime zest, for sprinkling on the tops of the cookies

Preheat the oven to 400°F (205°C). Line two baking sheets with parchment paper.

To make the cookies, in a large bowl, cream the butter and the sugar until light and fluffy. Add the egg, coconut extract and lime zest and juice. Sprinkle the salt and baking powder over the dough. Mix for 1 minute. Gently stir in the flour. Drop the dough by teaspoonfuls onto the prepared baking sheets, spacing 2 inches (5 cm) apart. You should have about 28 cookies. Bake for 5 to 7 minutes, or until just set and beginning to brown on the edges. Let the cookies cool for 5 minutes. Carefully remove to a rack. The cookies will be very soft.

Prepare the glaze by combining the powdered sugar, lime juice and coconut extract. Spoon the glaze over the warm cookies and sprinkle with the coconut and lime zest.

MUDDY BUDDY COOKIES

If you've never had a muddy buddy, they're a cereal treat that has peanut butter, chocolate and a thick coating of powdered sugar. Some people call them puppy chow, in case you know them by that name.

We all adore Sailor's best friend Paige. She's our unofficial adopted family member. Once when Sailor was having a bad day Paige made her a big batch of muddy buddies, but on the way to drop them off at our house, Paige ate almost all of them herself. Now you can see why we all love her so much—she fits right in with our treat-loving family. These cookies are for you, Paige. If you ask Paige what her favorite cookie is, she'll tell you it's any cookie that Sailor makes. Sailor is the one that came up with this recipe for muddy buddy–loving Paige, and many, many other recipes that you'll find in this book.

Makes 24 cookies

10 tbsp (140 g) unsalted butter, softened

½ cup (110 g) light brown sugar, packed

½ cup (100 g) granulated sugar

1 egg

½ tsp vanilla extract

½ tsp salt

½ tsp baking powder

½ tsp baking soda

½ cup (44 g) cocoa powder

1¼ cups (156 g) all-purpose flour

½ cup (84 g) peanut butter chips, plus more for the tops

¾ cup (30 g) muddy buddies, such as Chex Muddy Buddies, crushed, plus more for the tops

2 (1.55-oz [42-g]) milk chocolate bars, such as Hershey Bars, roughly chopped, divided

Preheat the oven to 350°F (175°C). Line two baking sheets with parchment paper.

In a large bowl, cream together the butter, brown sugar and granulated sugar until light and fluffy. Add the egg and vanilla. Sprinkle the salt, baking powder, baking soda and cocoa powder over the dough. Mix until no lumps remain. Gently stir in the flour. Fold in the peanut butter chips, muddy buddies and half of the chocolate pieces. Roll the dough into ping-pong-sized balls. Place on the prepared baking sheets about 2 inches (5 cm) apart.

Bake for 7 to 8 minutes, or until just set. Do not overbake. Remove from the oven and immediately poke the additional peanut butter chips, muddy buddies and remaining chocolate pieces into the tops of the cookies. Let the cookies cool on the baking sheets for 10 minutes before transferring to a rack to cool completely.

SOFT PUMPKIN
MILK CHOCOLATE CHIP COOKIES

I can hardly wait for fall for a chance to bake these pumpkin cookies. I like to really taste the pumpkin in my cookies, so I keep the spices light, but you can double them if you want a warmer, spiced flavor—or leave the spices out altogether, as per my P.S. below.

The secret to the best pumpkin cookie is to not add an egg since the pumpkin works as an egg substitute, in addition to flavoring and softening the cookie. This cookie is an easy one to convert to vegan. Just use vegan butter and dairy-free chocolate chips. However you make these cookies, keep in mind that they are delicious warm from the oven, but I think they are even better on the second day when the flavors have had a chance to fully develop.

P.S. You might consider leaving out all of the spices if you want the pumpkin flavor to come through with more oomph.

Makes about 24 cookies

⅓ cup (80 ml) pumpkin puree

½ cup (114 g) unsalted butter, softened

⅔ cup (132 g) granulated sugar

3 tbsp (42 g) brown sugar, packed

1½ tsp (8 ml) vanilla extract

½ tsp cinnamon

¼ tsp cloves

¼ tsp cardamom

Pinch of nutmeg

¾ tsp salt

½ tsp baking powder

1 tsp baking soda

1½ cups (188 g) all-purpose flour

1 cup (168 g) chocolate chips, divided

Line a strainer with a double layer of paper towels. Spread the pumpkin over the paper towels and let it drain, over a bowl, for 10 minutes.

Preheat the oven to 350°F (175°C). Line two baking sheets with parchment paper and lightly coat with cooking spray.

In a large bowl, cream together the butter, granulated sugar and brown sugar until light and fluffy. Stir in the pumpkin and vanilla. The dough might look streaky and separated, but it will come back together. Add the cinnamon, cloves, cardamom, nutmeg, salt, baking powder and baking soda. Stir until well combined. Gently stir in the flour. Add ⅔ cup (111 g) of the chocolate chips. Let the dough rest for 15 minutes. Drop the dough by rounded tablespoonfuls (14 g) onto the prepared baking sheets, spacing 2 inches (5 cm) apart. You should have 24 cookies.

The cookies will be irregularly shaped and craggy. If you want them to be more uniform in appearance, chill the dough for 1 hour, roll into balls, flatten slightly with your fingertips and bake as directed.

Bake for 7 to 9 minutes, or just until the tops are beginning to turn golden brown. Immediately poke 4 or 5 chocolate chips into the top of each cookie, pushing down to deflate the cookies a little since they will be puffy. Let the cookies cool for 10 minutes on the baking sheets before transferring to a rack to cool completely.

AMARETTI

Italian cookies won't always grab your visual attention because they usually aren't big show-offs like American cookies. Instead, they are usually small and unassuming, but nonetheless balanced and delicious. These assertive little almond-flavored Italian cookies are easy to make and delicious to eat. I had them for the first time on a trip to Florence many years ago, and I almost ignored them because I didn't see any chocolate. They're naturally gluten-free since the flour is made from ground almonds.

Makes 30 cookies

2 cups (188 g) almond flour

¼ tsp salt

1 cup (200 g) granulated sugar

1 tsp almond extract

1 tsp vanilla extract

2 egg whites

¾ cup (90 g) powdered sugar

Preheat the oven to 325°F (165°C). Line two baking sheets with parchment paper.

In a large bowl, with a wooden spoon, combine the flour, salt and sugar. Stir in the almond extract, vanilla and egg whites until the mixture is well combined. If the mixture is too dry, add a tablespoon (15 ml) of water. Shape the cookie dough into 30 (1-inch [2.5-cm]) balls. Roll each ball in the powdered sugar and place on the prepared baking sheets with 2 inches (5 cm) of space between the cookies.

Bake for about 25 minutes, or until golden brown. The cookies will be chewy for the first day, and will become crispier by the second day, so plan accordingly based on your preference. I like them both ways! Store cookies in an airtight container for up to a week.

MOM'S CHOCOLATE CHIP SHORTBREAD

These simple little cookies would make a lovely after-school snack for kids,
or a lovely midafternoon treat for grown-ups. I love the little hint or orange, but if you want
to keep it straightforward and simple, just omit the orange zest and maybe add a little vanilla.
I like these little cookies cut into triangles or squares, but you could
also roll them into balls and flatten for a round cookie.

Makes 16 cookies

⅔ cup (150 g) unsalted butter, softened

½ cup (60 g) powdered sugar

1 tsp orange zest, optional

1½ cups (188 g) all-purpose flour

¾ cup (126 g) miniature chocolate chips

½ cup (100 g) granulated sugar

Preheat the oven to 350°F (175°C). Line a baking sheet with parchment paper.

In a large bowl, cream together the butter and sugar until light and fluffy. Add the orange zest, if using, and flour. Mix gently. Stir in the chocolate chips. Pat the dough into an 8 x 8-inch (20 x 20-cm) square, then cut the cookies into 2 x 2-inch (5 x 5-cm) squares. Place on the prepared baking sheet about 1 inch (2.5 cm) apart. Sprinkle the tops of the cookies with the granulated sugar.

Bake for 8 to 10 minutes, or until just beginning to brown. Let the cookies cool on the baking sheet for 5 minutes before removing to a rack to cool completely.

ORANGE-FROSTED CARROT COOKIES

No one can say where this cookie came from. It just appeared in mothers' and grandmothers' recipe files many decades ago. You don't see it around too much anymore, edged-out by pushier, flashier cookies. But this shouldn't be! These are one of my favorite springtime cookies.

The flavor is so buttery, with a fresh hit of citrus from the orange frosting. And yes, there's carrot in there, but you've had carrot cake and you know what a delicate sweetness carrots can add to your baked goods. If you haven't tried these old-fashioned favorite cookies, you're in for a surprisingly wonderful treat. I'm making a pitch to bring them back into fashion.

Makes 32 cookies

COOKIES

1 cup (227 g) unsalted butter, softened, or use vegetable shortening as the original recipe calls for

¾ cup (150 g) granulated sugar

1 cup (228 g) cooked, mashed carrots

1 egg

1 tsp vanilla extract

½ tsp salt

2 tsp (9 g) baking powder

2 cups (250 g) all-purpose flour

GLAZE

1 tbsp (14 g) unsalted butter, softened

Zest and juice from 1 small fresh orange

2 cups (240 g) powdered sugar

Preheat the oven to 375°F (190°C). Line two baking sheets with parchment paper.

To make the cookies, in a large bowl, cream together the butter and sugar until light and fluffy. Stir in the carrots, egg and vanilla. Sprinkle the salt and baking powder over the batter and stir for 1 minute. Add the flour, stirring gently, until just combined. Drop by rounded tablespoonfuls (14 g) onto the baking sheets. You should have 32 cookies.

Bake for 8 to 10 minutes, or until just beginning to turn golden brown. Let the cookies cool on the baking sheets for 5 minutes and then transfer to a rack to cool completely.

Prepare the glaze by combining the butter and orange zest and juice. Stir in the sugar to form a thick glaze. Frost the cooled cookies and serve, or wait an hour or so until the glaze sets, if you like. These will stay fresh and soft for up to a week in an airtight container.

PECAN PIE SQUARES

My little ninety-year old neighbor Ramona has a big, beautiful pecan tree that she planted when she was a young bride many decades ago. Every year she brings my family mountains of buttery pecans. It gives me a chance to make these family favorite Pecan Pie Squares. These are a cross between a pie and a cookie, with a sturdy shortbread crust and a filling that will remind you of a luscious pecan pie with a hint of chocolate.

Makes 32 squares

CRUST

2 cups (250 g) all-purpose flour

⅓ cup (66 g) granulated sugar

½ tsp salt

¾ cup (170 g) unsalted butter, cold

FILLING

4 large eggs, room temperature

1½ cups (360 ml) corn syrup

1½ cups (300 g) granulated sugar

3 tbsp (42 g) unsalted butter, melted

2 tsp (10 ml) vanilla extract

¼ tsp salt

2¼ cups (245 g) chopped pecans

1 cup (168 g) miniature semisweet chocolate chips, optional

Preheat the oven to 350°F (175°C). Line a 15 x 10 x 1-inch (38 x 25 x 2.5-cm) jelly roll pan with parchment paper, leaving a little extra on both sides to create handles for lifting out the bars when they are ready to cut.

To make the crust, in a large bowl, combine the flour, sugar and salt. Using a box grater, grate the butter over the top and stir to combine. Press the mixture into the prepared baking pan. Bake the crust for 20 minutes, or until just starting to brown.

Meanwhile, to make the filling, in a large bowl, whisk the eggs, corn syrup, sugar, butter, vanilla and salt until thoroughly combined. Fold in the pecans and the chocolate chips, if using. Pour the pecan mixture over the hot crust and bake for 28 to 34 minutes, or until the filling is set. Remove from the oven and place the jelly roll pan on a rack to cool. To get the prettiest bars, refrigerate for at least 2 hours before cutting.

CARAMEL COCONUT CASHEW COOKIES

I brought these cookies to a big Italian family dinner, and they were devoured as I walked through the door. The next time I tried to make them I was down to the end of my cashew jar. I used cashews in a third of the cookies, macadamia nuts in another third and pecans in the remaining cookies. Little did I know that this would cause a temporary war in the family. Everyone had an opinion about which nut was best. Personally, I like the salty roasted cashews, but please—*per favore*—don't fight with me. You can use whatever nut you like.

Makes 24 cookies

½ cup (114 g) unsalted butter, softened

½ cup (110 g) dark brown sugar, packed

⅓ cup (66 g) granulated sugar

1 tsp coconut extract

1 egg

¼ tsp salt

¼ tsp baking powder

½ tsp baking soda

1½ cups (168 g) all-purpose flour

½ cup (47 g) unsweetened coconut flakes

1 cup (168 g) caramel baking chips

¾ cup (97 g) salted roasted cashews, coarsely chopped

Preheat the oven to 350°F (175°C). Line two baking sheets with parchment paper.

In a large bowl, cream together the butter, dark brown sugar and granulated sugar until light and fluffy. Add the coconut extract and egg. Sprinkle the salt, baking powder and baking soda over the top. Mix well. Gently stir in the flour. Fold in the coconut, baking chips and cashews. Roll the cookies into balls, using 2 tablespoons (28 g) of dough for each one. Place on the prepared cookie sheets about 2 inches (5 cm) apart.

Bake for 7 to 9 minutes, or until just set. Let the cookies cool on the baking sheets for 5 minutes before removing to a rack to cool completely.

CHOCOLATE BROWNIE MERINGUES

When I want a chocolaty treat that's a little on the lighter side, this is my go-to cookie. This little meringue packs a lot of chocolate flavor with both cocoa powder in the batter and on top, and also miniature chocolate chips inside. These are crunchy and chewy and intensely satisfying—even for those that don't care if a treat is light or decadent. The cocoa powder will cause the meringues to rise up and collapse a little, creating a chewy, fudgy texture that helps reinforce the brownie taste. These were one of my most popular cookies on my Instagram account, and it's not hard to see—or taste—why. See below for a Christmas variation that's a bit like a peppermint bark meringue.

Makes about 36 meringues

4 egg whites, room temperature

½ tsp vanilla

¼ tsp cream of tartar

Pinch of salt

½ cup (100 g) granulated sugar

¼ cup (22 g) cocoa powder, plus more for sprinkling on top

½ cup (60 g) powdered sugar

½ cup (84 g) miniature chocolate chips

¼ cup (27 g) chopped pecans

Preheat the oven to 225°F (110°C). Line two baking sheets with parchment paper.

In a large bowl, using a handheld or free-standing mixer, beat the egg whites and vanilla until foamy. Add the cream of tartar and pinch of salt, beating until the egg whites form soft peaks. This will take a few moments. The mixture should be white and puffy, but not hold a stiff shape. Continue to beat the mixture, gradually adding the granulated sugar, a tablespoon (15 g) at a time. Beat until the mixture holds stiff peaks. A good way to test when the mixture is ready is to turn your whisk upside down with some of the meringue on the tip. The mixture should hold its stiff shape when you turn the beater upside down. Turn off the mixer and set the mixture aside.

In a separate bowl, sift the cocoa powder and powdered sugar. With a rubber spatula, gently stir the cocoa powder and powdered sugar into the egg white mixture until well combined. Stir in the chocolate chips and pecans. Spoon the mixture in small amounts, about a tablespoon (14 g) each, onto the prepared baking sheets. You should form between 32 and 40 cookies. Sprinkle the tops with cocoa powder.

Bake the cookies for 1 hour. Turn off the oven and let the meringues rest in the oven for 1 hour. Remove from the oven and cool completely on the cookie sheets. The cookies are ready to eat when they are completely cooled and crisp.

Christmas Variation: *Swap out the pecans for an equal amount of crushed peppermint candy canes. Dip the bottoms of the finished meringues in melted white chocolate and sprinkle the edges of the white chocolate with more crushed candy canes.*

A BAKER'S DOZEN THANK YOUS

The first thank you goes to Sailor Elizabeth Mylroie, the girl who was involved with every step of the process. Her name is on the dedication page, and her name goes first here. I can't thank her enough in writing, so I'm sure I will find a more tangible way to express my appreciation. A trip, Sailor? What do you say?

To Shane, for taking over all the unpleasant, boring tasks of life for this season, so that I could do the pleasant, exciting and creative ones—like writing this book. It's your turn now, Shane. What do you want to do?

To West, who had to try cookies all day long, even when he didn't want to anymore, even when he was trying to get abs at the gym, even after he had just brushed his teeth. I will go back to making real food and not just cookies for my growing boy again, including tacos with deep-fried shells, like he keeps requesting.

To my dad, who will be the first one to buy dozens of copies of my book. That's how my dad is. He's always on the front row of the bleachers when someone he loves is playing the game. I don't know how he manages to make so many people feel supported, but I'm always glad to count myself as one of them. P.S. If you know my dad, he probably already pre-ordered you a cookbook.

To my mom, who taught me to bake. One of my first memories is baking cookies with my mom on my third birthday. I still remember the green, old-fashioned cookie presses and the special, warm and comforting feeling of being in the kitchen with my mother. Thank you for those wonderful memories.

To my sisters, I will never accomplish anything of value without running it by them first, all seven of them. When I have moments of self-doubt, they always believe in me. Sometimes I'm not even sure why or how, but their confidence in me is a source of strength without which I simply could not manage. People say it's rough being a middle child, but when it comes to sibling support, I say it is the best spot of all. To my sisters, I promise that I'll talk about something else besides cookies soon. I'm still going to talk about cookies, of course, but maybe a few other topics too.

To my pesky little brothers, just because. I love them both, but don't tell them I said so. P.S. They didn't help me at all. Typical little brothers. Hee hee.

To my niece Eloise, for testing recipes with exactness and providing feedback. You'd be hard-pressed to find a more amiable baker or person. She is always welcome in my kitchen. I probably still owe her some money.

To two more nieces, Sunny and Lavender, who wrote down over one hundred cookie recipe ideas on crumpled scratch paper, in the desperate hope of getting their names printed in this cookbook. There you go, guys. You hit the big time now.

To my Instagram family, the hardest part about writing a cookbook for me is holding back recipes from my IG family until publication. I want to share all my best food with you. Even if a screen separates us, you are real friends to me. I wish I could give you all a fresh, warm cookie in appreciation.

To my copy editors, especially the brilliant Sidonie. I hope I'm getting better at catching my own typos and errors, but it wouldn't be good enough without your careful eyes on my work. Thank you for helping me make the book something to be proud of.

To Ekaterina, for taking beautiful photos of cookies and for patiently helping me catch any recipes that needed clarification. Ekaterina's photo of the Nutella Lava Cookies still blows me away every time I see it. Gorgeous!

Finally, to Marissa, Meg and Will at Page Street Publishing, for giving me this dream-come-true opportunity. It's a lot of work—more than you might imagine—to write a cookbook, or make any kind of dream come true, I suspect, but it's the best kind of work. I'm so grateful to be able to do it. Thank you, Marissa and Meg, for guiding me along the way.

ABOUT THE AUTHOR

Erin Renouf Mylroie is a history and humanities professor by day, and a recipe developer and Instagrammer by night. Her passions include travel, poetry, crossword puzzles, fitness, healthy meals and decadent treats—especially cookies! Erin is the author of *2-Ingredient Miracle Dough Cookbook*. She has shared her award-winning recipes on the Food Network, *The Rachael Ray Show* and *Studio 5*, where she is a regular contributor, as well as in several publications, such as *Better Homes and Gardens*, *Bon Appetit*, *Cooking Light* and *Woman's Day* magazine. She lives in southern Utah with her husband and two children.

INDEX